Praise for the *Cruxio Bridge Quick-Start Guide*

"The Cruxio Bridge model has achieved ***remarkable results*** for me over the past ten years. It has enabled me to convince the Novartis Executive Committee and Board of Directors to act on multiple occasions, and at Moderna, I have used the model to engage internal and external stakeholders in the rapid development of a vaccine for SARS CoV 19.

"I wholeheartedly recommend the *Cruxio Bridge Quick-Start Guide*—it will help you master the art of persuasion!"

—Juan Andres, Chief Technical Operations, Moderna Therapeutics

"I have created multiple stories using the Cruxio Bridge model. The practical results that each story produces convince me of this method's power. This book reveals the underlying magic that creates clearly ***structured, persuasive, action-oriented*** stories. Learn and apply the magic—I have found it transformational!"

—Dr. Pierre-Alain Ruffieux, CEO, Lonza Group Ltd.

"I used to struggle to build a clear, compelling story that would produce the outcomes I wanted. Applying the Cruxio Bridge model over recent years has completely changed that. Now, my messages land with ***more impact*** and I go into high-stakes settings more confident of achieving the desired result.

"*The Cruxio Bridge Quick-Start Guide* will show you how to structure and pressure-test your ideas, making you a more effective and influential communicator."

—Jerry Cacia, Genentech Executive Committee Member

"I highly recommend the Cruxio Bridge model to executives, scientists, and anyone who needs to persuade others to support advancing their ideas and dreams—just as it has done for me!"

—Dr. Kevin Forrest, CEO, Expansion Therapeutics

"When you endeavor to ***inspire others***, your credibility is at stake. Following the robust Cruxio Bridge model safeguards your credibility and creates powerful, convincing messages that will convert your dreams into tangible action. I continue to have my top talent trained in the Cruxio Bridge process because it results in clearer communication, thinking, and decision-making."

—Adriana Rubio, President, Roche Diagnostics Latin America

"Since 2007, and to this day, Cruxio has taught its methodologies to Stanford University's Innovation fellows from the Byers Center for Biodesign. Many of the fellows are physicians and engineers new to the idea of pitching to investors—a key element of the program. Consistently, the learning transformed their pitches: they became ***sharper, more engaging, and persuasive***."

—Dr. Todd Brinton, Fellowship Director (2006–2019), Stanford Byers Center for Biodesign

The Cruxio Bridge

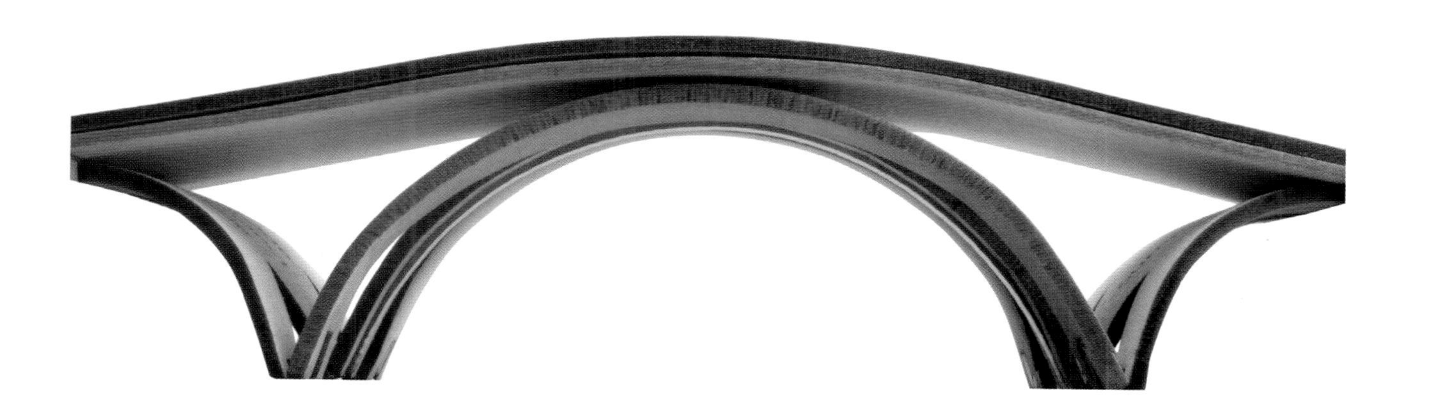

Quick-Start Guide

The Cruxio Bridge

Build Persuasive Communications that **Motivate Action**

Rob Wishnowsky

The Cruxio Bridge®

The Cruxio Bridge by Rob Wishnowsky

Published by Cruxio Media

ISBN: 978-1-7336917-0-3 (Hardback)
ISBN: 978-1-7336917-1-0 (Paperback)
ISBN: 978-1-7336917-2-7 (Ebook)

Examples provided in this book are fictitious, disguised, or composites of different situations. All are based on realities experienced over 37 years of working with, and within, corporations.

Book and cover design by DesignForBooks.com

Printed in China.

For my mother, Norma, and Wendy—my soulmate.

Contents

List of figures

Acknowledgments

I am grateful to Garrett Boon, a model bridge maker based in Montana, whose encyclopedic mind led me to the Norwegian interpretation of Leonardo da Vinci's bridge. With his creative help, woodworking skills, and a generous dollop of patience, Garrett enabled us to take the Cruxio Bridge from prototype in November 2017 to small-scale production in June 2019.

More than a decade ago, Juan Andres took a leap of faith by developing a critically important presentation with this methodology. Thank you for your trust, Juan, and for leading me into the fascinating (and complex!) field of drug manufacturing. It was there that I met Dr. Pierre-Alain Ruffieux who, despite running a huge organization, made time to periodically review the developing manuscript. It is stronger as a result; thank you!

This book wouldn't be in your hands without steady encouragement and honest critique from my wife, Wendy. Thank you, my love! Niveet and my daughter, Anna, also provided helpful critique in the early stages of this project.

Since starting Cruxio fifteen years ago, I have relied on professional help to do what I cannot. I greatly appreciate the services of the experts who helped this novice navigate the world of publishing. Special thanks to Michael Rohani for challenging an earlier structure of this book and to Eric Stampfli, who had to shoot multiple versions of the Cruxio Bridge as it evolved!

Developmental editing

Rosemi Mederos

Michael Rohani

Copy editing

Judy Gruen

Tammy McCausland

Book design

Michael Rohani

Proofreading and index editing

Heather Pendley

Photography

Eric Stampfli (Cruxio Bridge model)

Stig Jarnes (Norwegian footbridge)

"Without good communication skills you won't be able to convince people to follow you, even though you see over the mountain and they don't."[1]

—Warren Buffett
CHAIRMAN AND CEO,
BERKSHIRE HATHAWAY

Poor communication devastates ideas and people.

Have you experienced the gut-wrenching disappointment of a failed pitch? If not, you must be new to the business world—welcome! However, if you present to senior-level business executives, you'll be familiar with some version of the following painful scene:

Late nights. Weekends.
Hundreds of hours.
Dozens of slides.
Review.
Revise.
Review.
Revise.

Pre-alignment meetings . . .
Tweak.
Tweak.
Tweak.

The big day. Your hour of opportunity!
The meeting's running late.
There's been heated debate.
Oh. Now you have only 20 minutes.
Twenty minutes before their delayed lunch.

Hungry. Angry.
Hangry *decision-makers.*

Your vision gets nods.
Your champion supports it!
Your budget gets frowns.
Your champion evaporates.

It's time for lunch.
Come back in six weeks with more data.
And a revised budget.

Now, whose is the gluten-free sandwich?

Sadly, this type of experience is common. As a result, great ideas are buried, careers stall, motivation is crushed. Everyone loses.

There's no doubt that persuading people in business is hard work, but that effort can be wasted unless it is also smart work—*strategically* smart. To get results and avoid devastating disappointment, focus first on your strategy. In these pages, you'll learn how Cruxio's strategic approach will motivate your audience to act!

Get action—approach business stories strategically

Your goal is action, not entertainment

"Storytelling" in business has been gaining traction in recent years. It sounds like a welcome direction for those of us who have suffered years of talking heads reading crowded slides to bored audiences. But, after spending more than a decade coaching executives to develop and deliver boardroom-level stories, the use of the word "storytelling" has me worried.

Why?

Because most of the stories we're exposed to are designed to entertain. Books, movies, TV shows, and stage plays are based on narrative forms. The shape of these stories—their arc—typically culminates in a high point of tension just before the story ends. As an audience, we are engaged by the conflicts and struggles that lead up to this climax and, ideally, we are satisfied or moved by their resolution.

About our company, Cruxio, Inc.

Our company's name is based both on the word "crux," which means "the essential point," and our business goal: to equip leaders to motivate action through persuasive stories. This explains our tagline, "the crux of the story."

Since 2005, clients have used our methodologies to secure more than $5 billion cumulatively to fund their initiatives. Four out of five executives return to work with us again. They return because they have experienced the value of thinking strategically about communications that are critical to their success. We have taught Cruxio's story development process to more than 1,000 businesspeople in workshops spanning the United States, Europe, South America, Asia, and New Zealand.

Great storytellers thoughtfully structure their stories to keep us on the hook right to the end. They are masters of entertainment. And there's the issue: the goal in the boardroom is to reach a decision, not to entertain. If you are presenting to a decision-level group, you are in the business of *persuasion.*

Business audiences want to know three things:

1. Why should I care?
2. Why should I believe you?
3. What do you want me to do?

The opening of an effective business story answers the first question. The middle, which comprises a robust set of arguments, answers the second question. The closing answers the third. You *should* approach your answers to these questions with a story mindset, but the structure and content of business stories are different from those in the entertainment worlds of stage, page, and screen. The approach you'll learn in these pages blends vital elements of entertaining stories such as challenges, conflict, and struggle, with the business essentials of data, facts, logic, and examples. Without challenges, conflict, and struggle, there is no story in entertainment. The same is true in business.

Here we lay out our strategic, step-by-step approach to building persuasive communications that motivate action. This approach can be applied to many types of communications, including:

Emails
Conversations
Presentations
Documents

We call these communications "strategic stories" because the thinking behind each story is fundamentally *strategic,* forms part of a communication *strategy,* and enables leaders to achieve *strategic* goals. Each story is tailored to a particular audience, which could be one key decision-maker, a committee of 10, or an audience of 100 or more people. Every strategic story is designed to improve a business by either starting a journey or continuing an existing journey toward a better future.

These journeys face barriers to progress that are like rivers that must be crossed. Tackling obstacles and overcoming challenges is difficult and risky, so people tend to resist! They're reluctant to make decisions in the face of uncertainty. They have competing priorities. Change is hard. Cruxio's strategic story development process equips you to surmount barriers to action, whether you are persuading others in the boardroom, in town hall meetings, or on the factory floor.

This book isn't about flashy presentations. It won't show you how to make sensational slides, but it will show you how to use the Cruxio process so that your openings seize your audience's attention, your arguments stand up to scrutiny, and your closing inspires action that catalyzes change, earns support for initiatives, or secures funding.

Conflict is central to strategic stories

Every strategic story is designed to answer a key question that you raise in the audience's minds. This question creates a conflict that the story must resolve. Here are examples of key questions raised within different types of strategic stories. The questions are expressed from the audience's point of view:

- In a pitch for investment funds, "Why should we believe that your start-up is likely to succeed when similar ones have failed?"
- In a board-level presentation, "Should we consider changing our strategy?"
- In an online training module, "How will this training help me in my job?"

Your message is the answer to the key question being asked. This singular focus gives the story a clear direction. You support your message with arguments. You close by asking your audience to act. The result is a simple three-part structure:

1. Opening
2. Arguments
3. Closing

1. Opening. In strategic stories, the opening raises a key question that matters to your audience (the question may be explicit or implicit). You answer it with your message, which states your position and shows the audience why they should care. This naturally leads to the arguments that support your message.

2. Arguments. The middle of the strategic story presents a set of arguments comprising data, facts, logic, and examples. These elements show the audience why they should believe your message and have confidence in you.

3. Closing. Your closing ties all your arguments together and asks the audience for specific action, either in that moment or in the future. This lets the business audience know what you want them to do.

Strategic stories speak rationally and emotionally

As businesspeople, we like to think of ourselves as being primarily rational, but research proves us wrong. Princeton University psychologist Daniel Kahneman won the 2002 Nobel Prize in Economics for demonstrating that our decisions aren't nearly as rational as we'd like to think.[2] Much additional research supports his profound insight that the main source of our explicit beliefs and deliberate choices are impressions and feelings.[3]

Stories speak to our emotional minds. This is another reason to approach persuasion in business with a story form. In multiple experiments, Kahneman has shown that people disregard even obvious data in favor of vivid descriptions. "No one ever made a decision because of a number," he said. "They need a story."[4]

"No one ever made a decision because of a number. They need a story."

—DANIEL KAHNEMAN, WINNER OF THE 2002 NOBEL PRIZE IN ECONOMICS

Leonardo da Vinci's bridge was (radically!) different

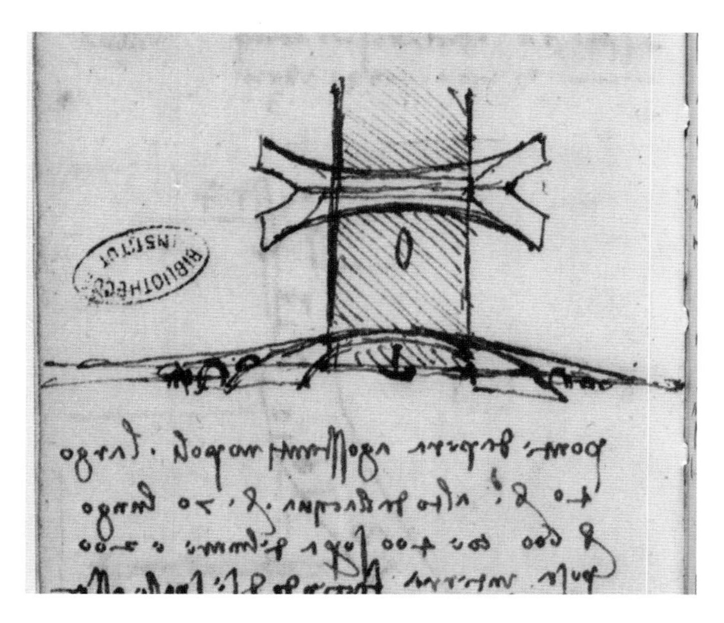

Leonardo da Vinci's sketches of the bridge show both a bird's-eye view and an elevation with a sailing ship passing beneath.

The wooden model Cruxio Bridge draws on a 1502 design by Leonardo da Vinci. His design would have solved a major problem for Sultan Bayezid II who wanted a bridge to span the Golden Horn inlet—connecting Istanbul with Galata—while still allowing tall sailing ships to pass into and out of the inlet. The usual solution of the era would have been a masonry bridge comprising a series of semicircular arches—at least ten in this case[5]—but that kind of construction would have prevented ships from passing.

Da Vinci envisioned a high, 900-foot (274 meters), single-span, parabolic arch sweeping across the Golden Horn. Built of stone and relying purely on compression for structural stability (no mortar) it would have been the longest bridge of its time.[6] It also would have worked![7]

Unfortunately for history and for us, the Sultan took a pass . . . but, 500 years later, da Vinci's design was brought to life as a bicycle and footbridge near Oslo, in Norway. The Norwegian interpretation features three arches that independently support the road above. These independent arches became a vital feature of the wooden model Cruxio Bridge.

Leonardo da Vinci inspired the Cruxio Bridge

This bicycle and footbridge in Norway is a one-third scale interpretation of Leonardo da Vinci's Golden Horn bridge design. The independent arches that you can see so clearly here inspired the design of the Cruxio Bridge model.

At Cruxio, we have used the metaphor of a bridge for years to represent how strategic stories enable business communicators to overcome obstacles on their path to a better future. The structure of these stories, and of the Cruxio Bridge, is specific: it's critical that arguments supporting a persuasive communication are independent of one another. Why? Because the failure of one argument does not necessarily mean the whole case will collapse, provided that the remaining arguments stand.

We searched for years to find a bridge design that would reflect this independent structure. When we saw the Norwegian interpretation of Leonardo da Vinci's Golden Horn bridge design, we knew we had found it. The independent arches could represent independent arguments that support the communicator's message. The roadway could represent the audience's experience. Finally, we had the basis of a physical model that would represent the key elements of a strategic story. In that moment, with deep thanks to Leonardo da Vinci, the Cruxio Bridge project was born!

Use the Cruxio Bridge

Learning through the senses

In business, we deal largely in abstractions—concepts that are neither concrete nor literal. We cannot see, hear, taste, or feel strategies, profits, or revenues. Before I entered this abstract world of business, I financed my microbiology degree in part by playing jazz piano and blues harmonica in a professional cabaret band. As a musician, I know that it is one thing to *think* about music, it is another to *listen* to it, and another to *make* it by plucking strings, playing a keyboard, or shaping a note through an instrument's mouthpiece. We remember things better when we engage our senses in learning.[8]

Knowing this fueled our quest to build a simple, elegant model bridge that could serve as an easily understood analogy, a visual reminder, and a tactile tool.* The resulting Cruxio Bridge comprises three sections that represent the beginning, middle, and

The Cruxio Bridge model emerged over a dozen years of working with clients to persuade decision-makers to act. The point of the model is that persuasion in business requires a strategic approach. The result is a clear, well-structured communication that connects with the audience rationally *and* emotionally.

*In addition to sight and touch, during a workshop we realized that the bridge also engages smell and hearing when a group of engineers held the bridge up to their noses to appreciate the natural wood and commented on the satisfying click as the box firmly closed!

end of your story. The model is built in three layers. The surface layer reflects the audience's experience. The layers beneath reflect the thinking you must do to shape their experience. The bridge design makes it easy to separate these sections and layers with your hands so that you see and feel the relationships between the key elements of a persuasive strategic story.

We remember things better when we engage our senses in learning.

The Cruxio Bridge model includes wooden tiles that serve as reminders of the step-by-step process needed to build your story. So, in one box you have the tiles, to remind you of the process, and the bridge, which shows you how the elements fit

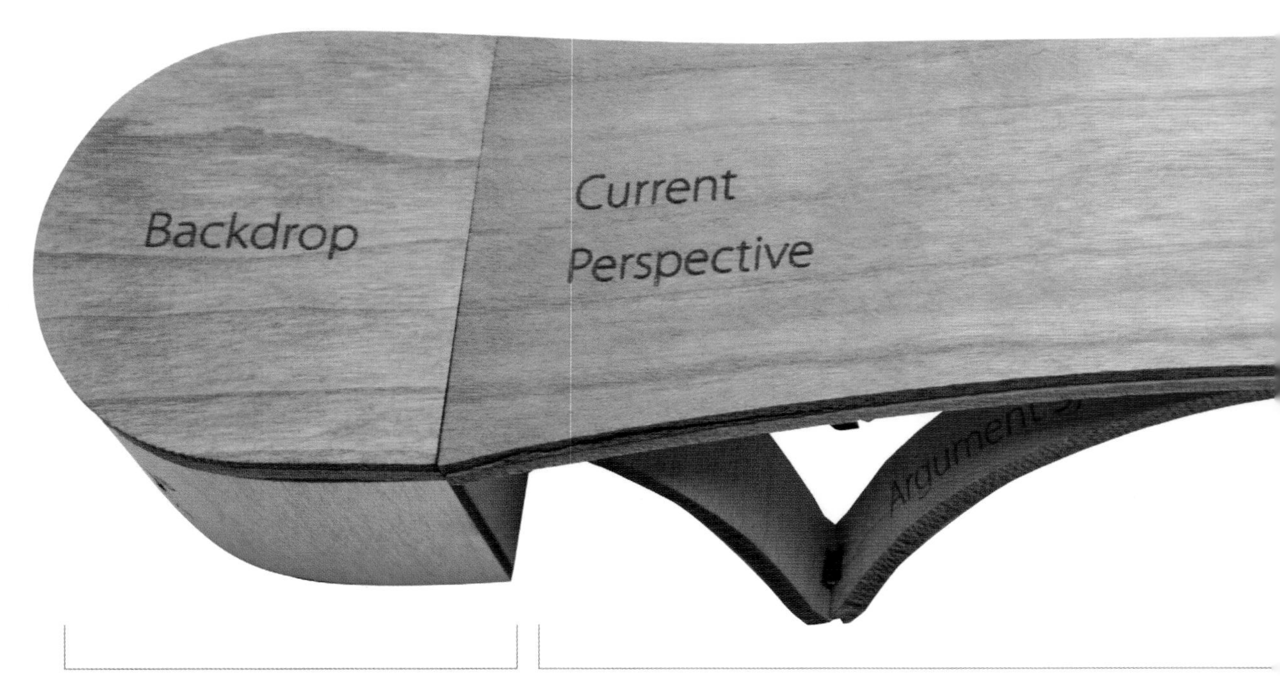

together. The model is a visual, physical metaphor that represents the structure of a strategic story.

Here's the metaphor. Your audience stands on one bank of a river (the bridge's on-ramp). You want them to cross to the other riverbank (the off-ramp) to be one stage closer to a better future that you envision—usually in the distance. By crossing, they are agreeing to take some action, such as approving and funding a proposal.

The river represents the audience's resistance to moving toward the better future. Your communication is a well-structured bridge that carries them over that resistance and offers them rewards for crossing. The audience will only cross if they trust you, trust your bridge, and see value in crossing to the other side.

Better Future

The better future you want to achieve may be months or even years away. The more clearly your audience can envision what it will look and feel like to be in this future, the more likely they are to support moving toward it.

Riverbank
(off-ramp)

The elements of the Cruxio Bridge model

The Cruxio Bridge model is connected magnetically between two riverbanks. The bridge is designed to flow from left to right. The surface of the left riverbank is labeled "Backdrop."

In theater, the stage is set against a backdrop that hangs at the back of the set, providing context for the foreground action. In the bridge model, the backdrop is a reminder to consider issues that may affect your audience's willingness to step onto the bridge. Your audience will view your strategic story in the context of *their* backdrop, so it's important that you anticipate factors from their perspective that could influence the success of your story.

Backdrop

Issues that may positively or negatively affect your audience's willingness to step onto the bridge form the backdrop of your strategic story. These issues may or may not be related to the better future you advocate.

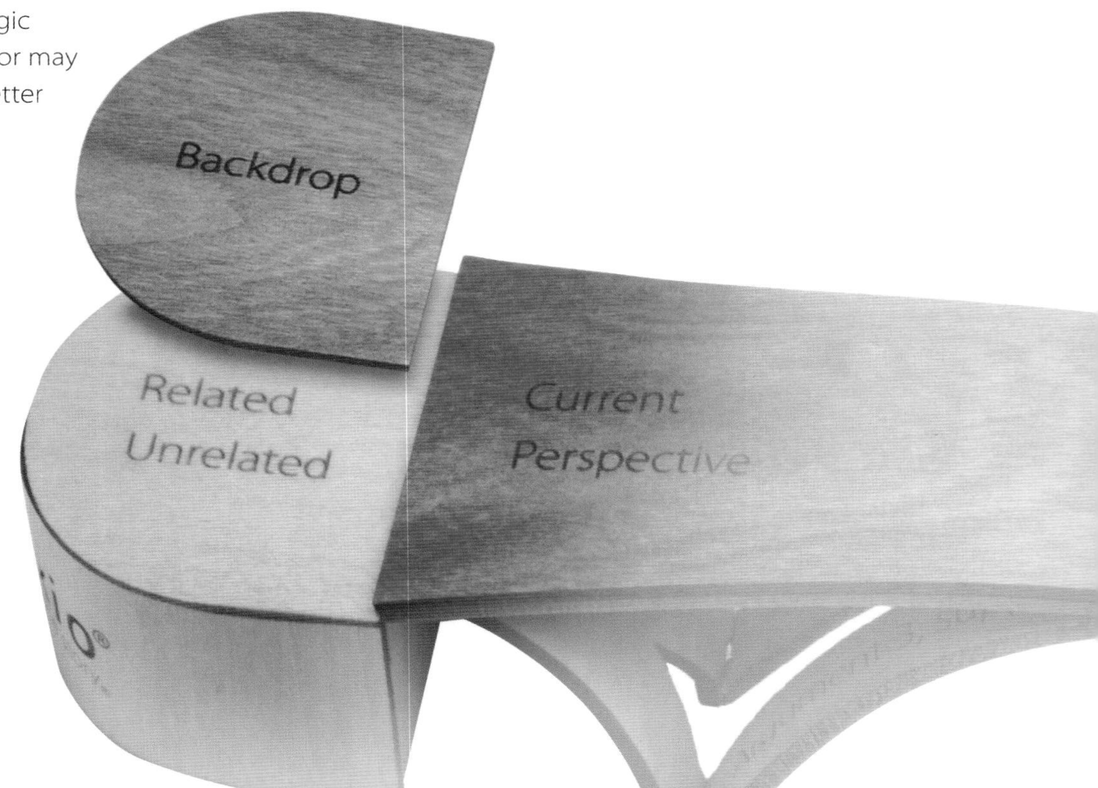

Issues may be related or unrelated to moving toward your proposed better future. *Related* backdrop issues include baggage such as past failures or unpopular initiatives. Pay attention if you hear, "We tried something like that; it didn't work." *Unrelated* issues can be broader, such as budget cuts or competing priorities. They can also be immediate issues, such as the audience being tired, hungry, or distracted. Remove the surface of the left riverbank and you'll see the words "Related" and "Unrelated" to remind you to be on the lookout for both kinds of backdrop issues.

Backdrop factors aren't always negative. For example, the better future you advocate could become more attractive due to recent changes or events. These positive factors can take many forms, such as funding windfalls or favorable changes in the regulatory environment.

The left surface of the bridge is labeled "Current Perspective" to remind you that as the audience steps onto your bridge, they will have their own expectations and views.

Those may differ from what you will communicate, but it's critically important that you anticipate their views, expectations, biases, preconceptions, and even misunderstandings.

The layer beneath "Current Perspective" is labeled "Thinking, Feeling, Doing." These words are reminders of how to anticipate your audience's current perspective. Ask yourself what they are likely to be thinking, feeling, and doing—if anything—related to your communication.

Current Perspective

What the audience is likely to be thinking, feeling, and doing—if anything—related to your anticipated communication.

The right surface of the bridge is labeled "New Perspective." This is the perspective that you want your audience to adopt at the end of your communication. The layer beneath is also labeled "Thinking, Feeling, Doing" to remind you how to determine the new perspective. It's the same idea: you need to anticipate what, *realistically,* you can expect the audience to be thinking, feeling, and doing as you bring your communication to a close.

New Perspective

What you want the audience to be thinking, feeling, and doing by the end of your communication.

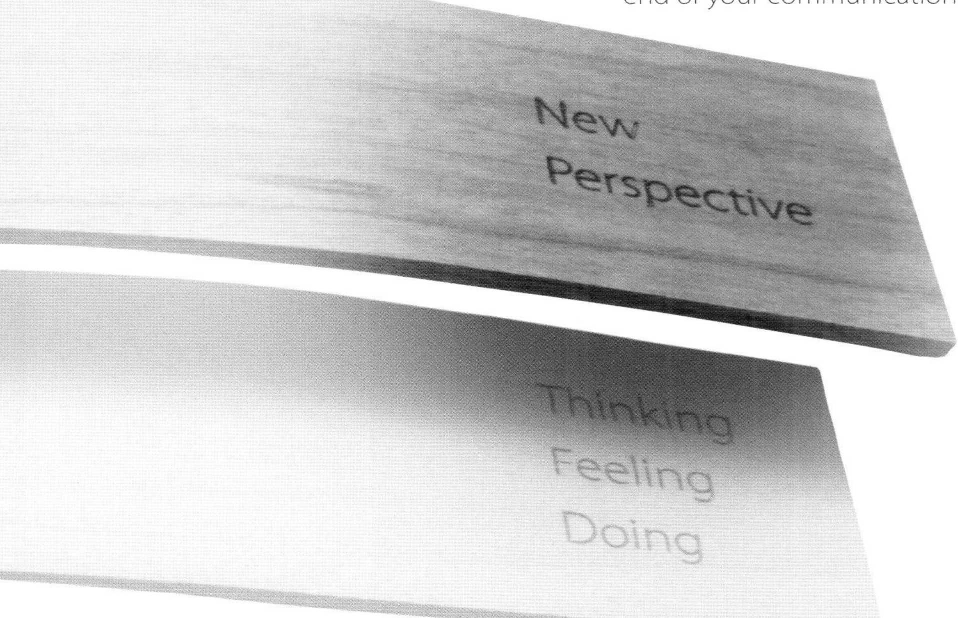

The surface of the right riverbank is labeled "Call to Action." As your audience steps off your bridge, you want them to do something. Strategic stories aren't just about persuasion, their goal is to get things done. Remove the riverbank surface and you'll

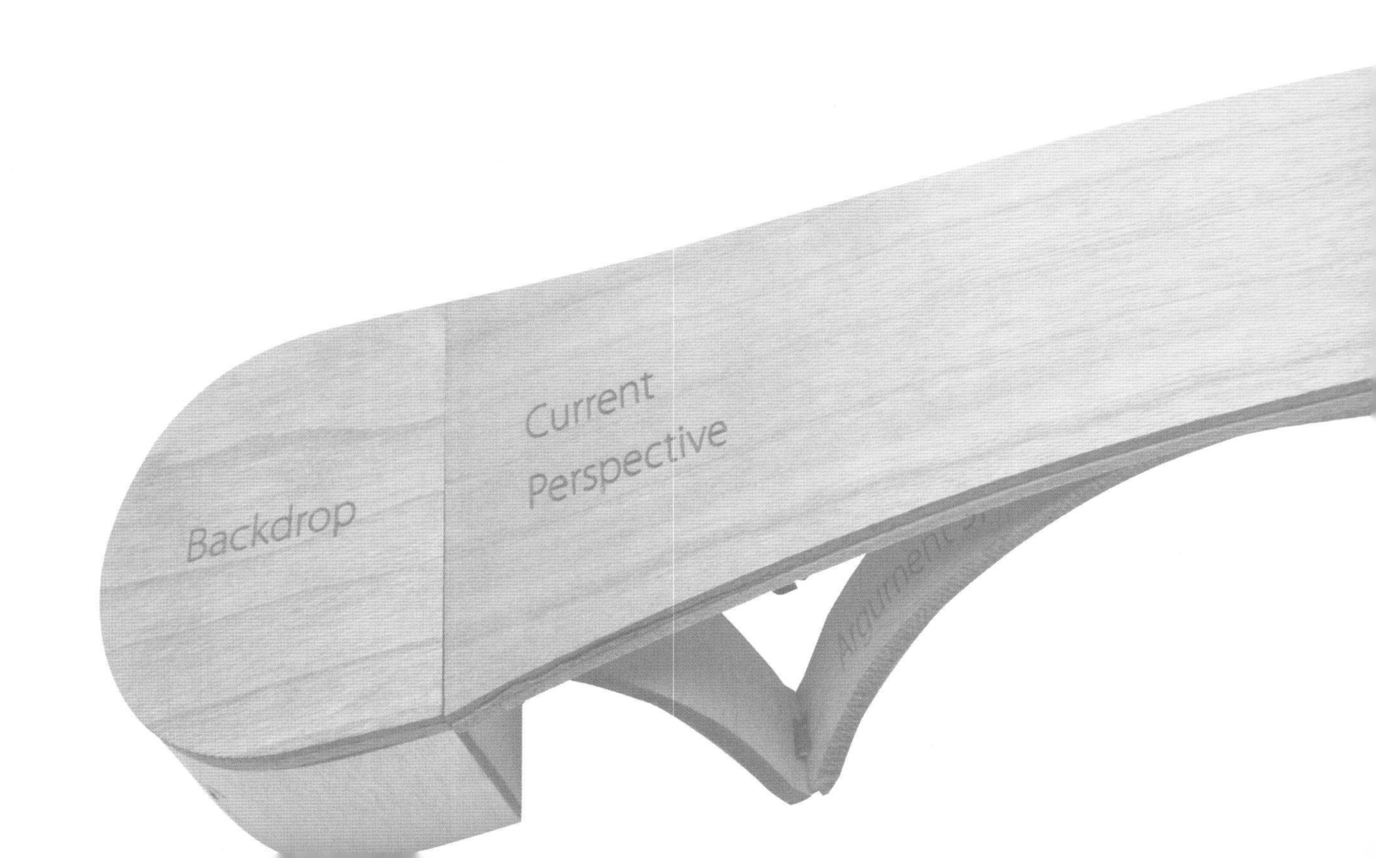

see "Be specific." This is a prompt to make your request specific, explicit, and actionable. Your audience can't act on generalities such as "Please endorse this project," but they can act on a specific request such as "Please approve $250,000 to fund stage one of this project."

Call to Action

The specific action(s) that you ask the audience to take once they have adopted the new perspective.

When assembled, the prominent view of the Cruxio Bridge is the cherrywood road surface, which reflects the audience's experience in crossing the bridge. The color contrast of this pretty cherrywood on top of the pale basswood is deliberate. Seeing this, and *not*

1 Leave behind backdrop issues.

2 Move away from their current perspective.

seeing all the work that lies beneath is a reminder to consistently consider your audience's experience.

To cross your bridge, they must go through a series of four rational and emotional changes. These changes will require them to:

3 Adopt the new perspective that you have proposed.

4 Agree to act in light of this new perspective.

Key elements of your opening

The opening of your strategic story is represented on the Cruxio Bridge by the backdrop and three words that are engraved on the bottom layer of the bridge: "Engage, Connect, Frame."

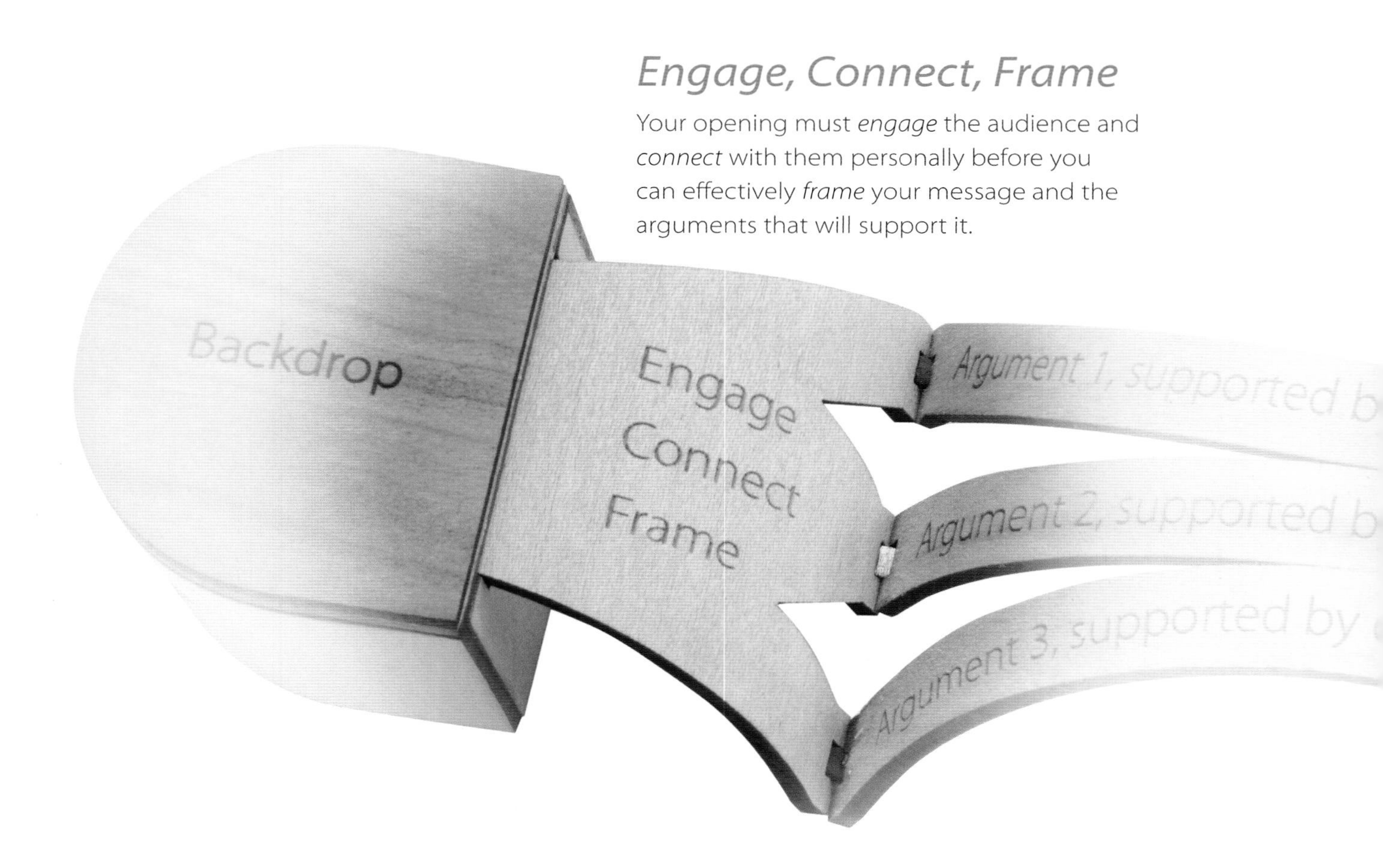

The backdrop is relevant because negative issues can be a barrier to progress until you acknowledge and address them. The three engraved words remind you to first *engage* your audience and *connect* with them personally before you *frame* your message and the arguments that will support it.

Engaging and connecting are vitally important because building relationships with your audience is essential to persuading them. Engaging your audience starts by seizing their attention and directing it toward your message. Connecting personally is critical because, as you'll see, people are persuaded in large part through emotions and relationships. One of our maxims at Cruxio is "Relationship is the foundation of persuasion." Yes, even in the cool, calm, calculated world of business!

Arguments support your message

Your success depends on persuading your audience to change their perspective. Your message, supported by robust arguments, enables this change.

In strategic stories, you usually state your message before unpacking the underlying arguments. Here's an example of a message: "We recommend investing $11 million now to expand our bottling plant to avoid the risk of losing $140 million in revenue next year." Naturally, your audience will want to understand the set of arguments that stand behind those numbers before agreeing to the investment.

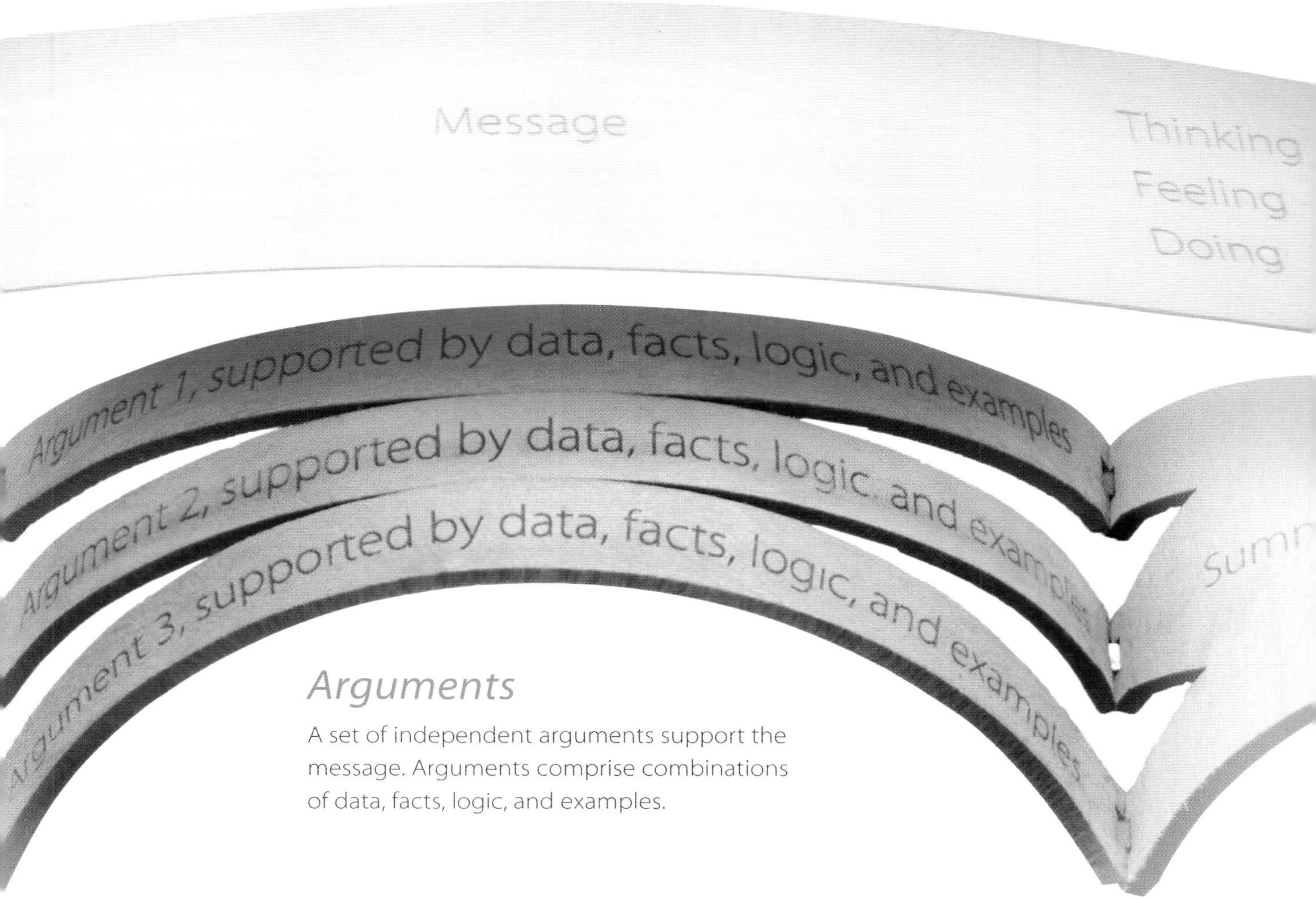

Arguments

A set of independent arguments support the message. Arguments comprise combinations of data, facts, logic, and examples.

The arguments are the load-bearing arches of the Cruxio Bridge. Since your arguments support your message, the word "Message" is engraved above them on the middle layer of the bridge.

As the bridge builder, most of your work is from bottom to top: arguments (bottom layer) support the message (middle layer), which together support the audience's change in perspective (top layer—the audience's experience).

The message has two important elements. First, it conveys your position, "We recommend investing $11 million now . . . " Second, it conveys why your proposal or idea matters—or should matter—to the audience, ". . . to avoid the risk of losing $140 million in revenue next year."

The bridge is designed so that each of the arguments—the bridge arches—independently supports the message. This independence is structurally important, just as it is in Norway's interpretation of Leonardo's design (page 6): the failure of one arch doesn't necessarily mean the bridge will fall.

Message

Your message is a brief statement of your position and why it should matter to the audience. It is the impetus for them to move from their current perspective to adopt the new perspective.

Similarly, if some in your audience don't buy one argument, the remaining arguments can still support your strategic story and your call to action. Arguments are made with data, facts, logic, and examples. These words are engraved on the arches of the bridge. The category of examples is broad, encompassing elements such as case studies, photos, videos, props, and narratives.

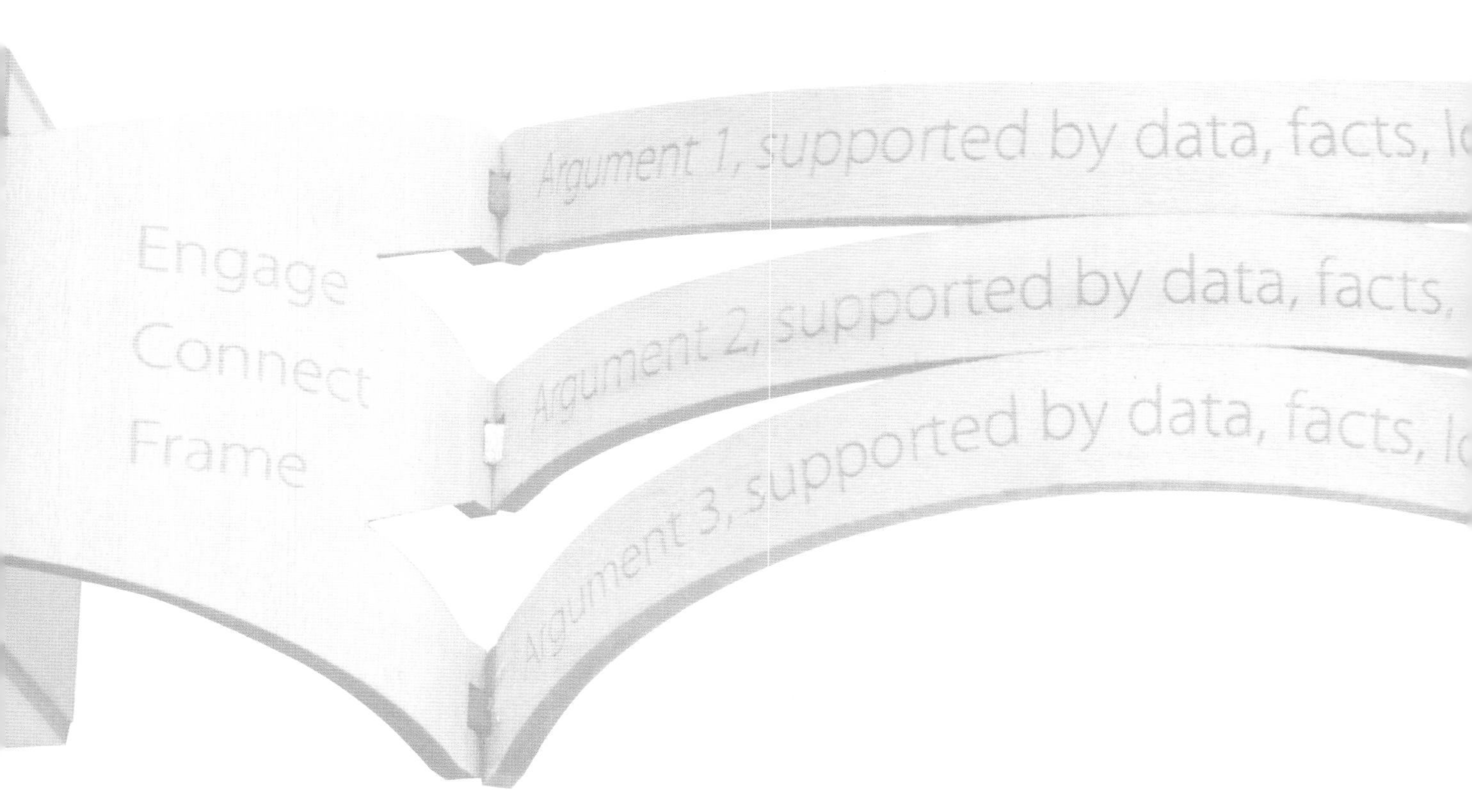

Key elements of your closing

Your summary is the beginning of your closing. To this point, your audience has heard (or read) your arguments sequentially; they haven't had a chance to consider them collectively. Your summary ties the arguments together in support of your message.

Summary

Your summary demonstrates the combined power of your arguments. It usually reprises rewards for adopting the new perspective and responding to your call to action.

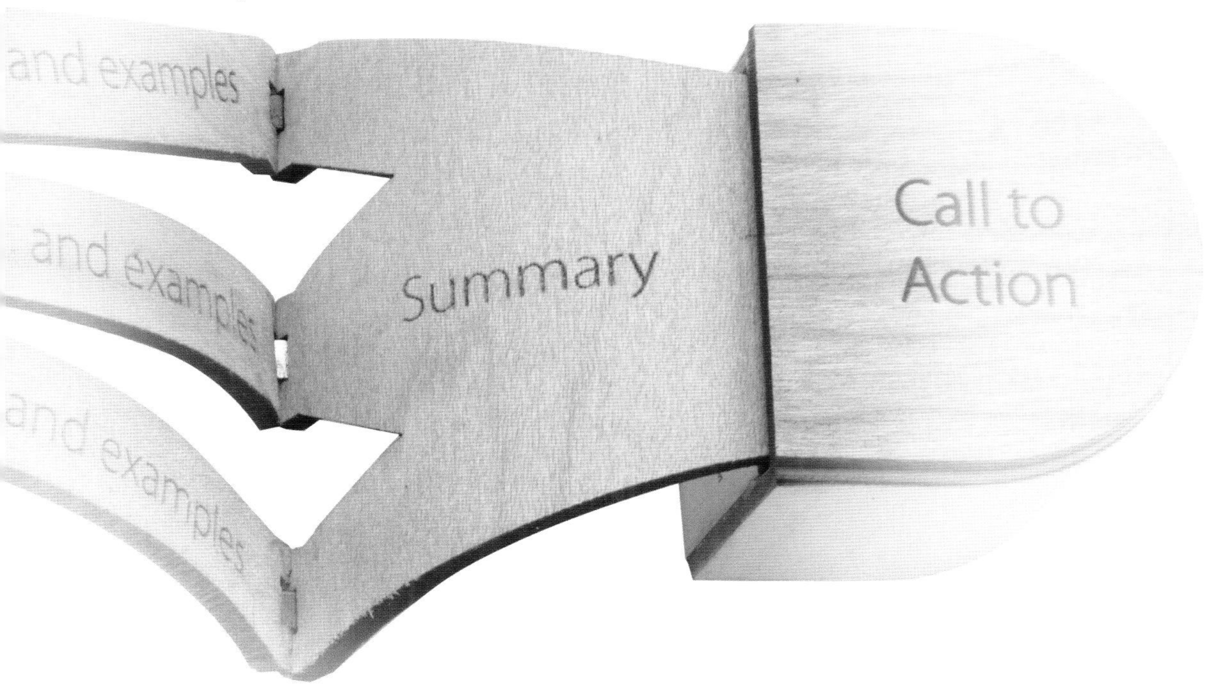

As you tie the arguments together, reprise your message and remind your audience of their rewards for crossing this bridge: the potential for them to gain, avoid pain, or both.

An effective summary leads to the call to action, which answers the audience's implicit question, "What do you want me to do?" These actions may be immediate or delayed. Examples of immediate action include approving funds for an initiative, scheduling the next meeting, or volunteering support in specific ways. A delayed action could be, "When you see this problem, do this, not that."

The Cruxio Bridge is a practical tool

The wooden bridge physically embodies the key elements of any persuasive business communication. Keep it in sight as a constant reminder to consider:

All participants in Cruxio's *"Persuasion Strategy"* workshops receive a copy of this Quick-Start Guide and a model Cruxio Bridge as a visual, tactile reminder of the process and key elements required to build a robust, persuasive strategic story.

- The context in which your message will be received.
- The change in perspective you will ask of the audience.
- Whether that change in perspective is truly realistic.
- How to engage the audience in your message.
- How to build a robust set of arguments.
- The rewards for crossing the bridge.
- Your specific call to action.

These factors are important whether you're writing an email or planning a board-level presentation.

The bridge is a framework, not a cookie-cutter formula. Although you'll follow the same process each time, the resulting stories will be different. The framework's value is that it helps you consistently create robust, clear, strategic stories.

The bridge helps you plan one stage of a journey to a better future

Imagine that you've applied for your dream job in a fantastic company. In your mind, you can see yourself in this role. You can imagine the personal development, fun, and satisfaction you'll gain from doing something that really matters. It will be great for your family, too! This is the better future that you envision.

There will be many stages and challenges in trying to achieve this better future. Stages are likely to include writing a compelling résumé and cover letter, phone or web interviews, and a series of in-person interviews with different people.

Similarly, to achieve strategic goals in business, you'll face a series of challenges. As in applying for your dream job, success depends on communicating effectively at each stage with different audiences. The Cruxio Bridge is designed to help you through each of these strategically important stages.

As Figure 1 illustrates, build the bridge you need for the current stage while anticipating the next one. This will help you develop your communication strategy. The better you can anticipate foreseeable stages, the more likely you are to reach the better future you envision.

"While the core flow of the process is consistent, thoughtful, and strategic, the resulting stories vary considerably. Each one has conveyed a distinctly honed message and produced successful outcomes."

—Dr. Kevin Judice
CEO, Dice Molecules

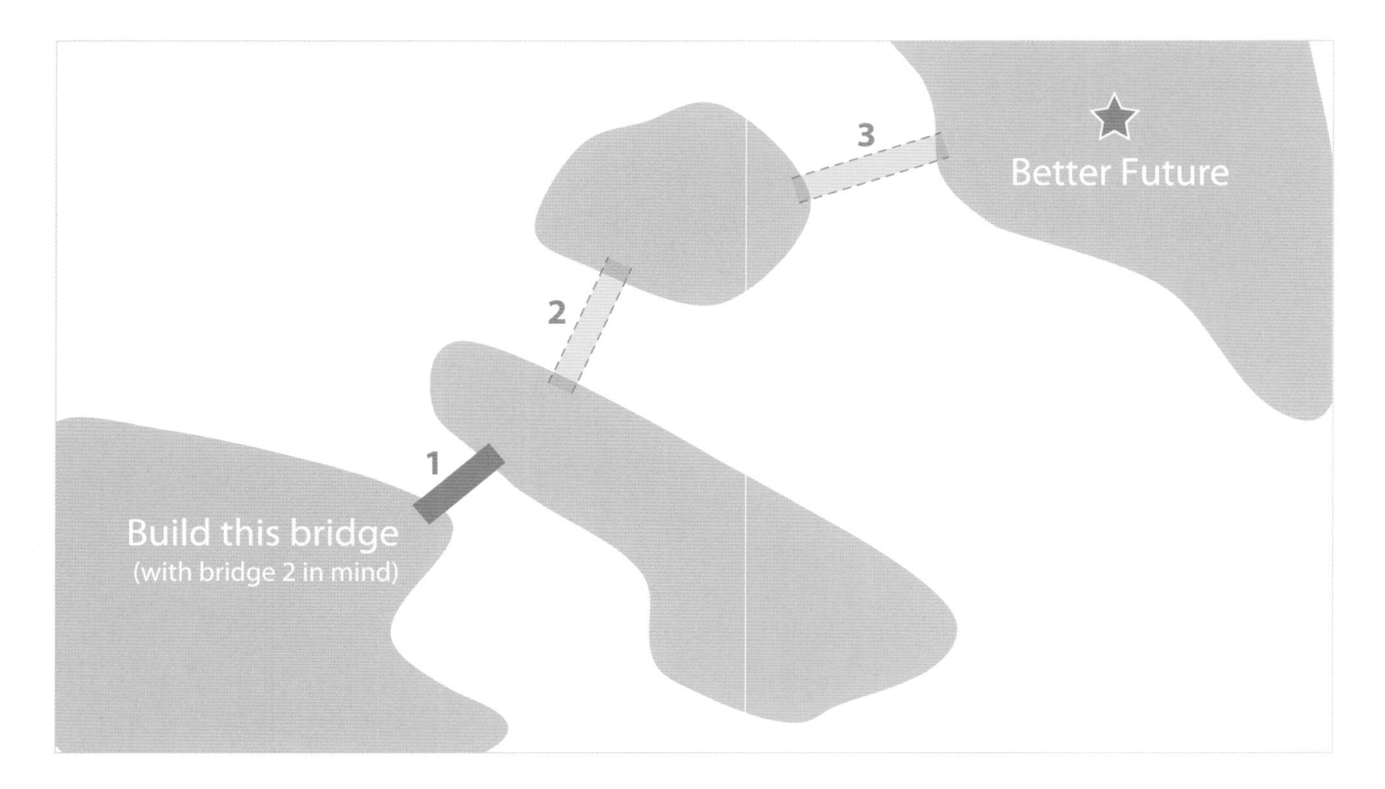

Figure 1: As you build your current bridge, anticipate the next stage or stages

You build a bridge step-by-step

A well-designed bridge creates a seamless, smooth passage from one side to the other. As a bridge-building communicator, your job is to enable your audience to smoothly exchange their current perspective for your proposed new perspective. To create that experience, a lot of your time will be spent beneath the surface, working bottom-up on the infrastructure. As with much bridge construction, you will assemble pieces toward the end of the project. That may sound counter-intuitive when the goal is to get from one side to the other, but it's dangerous to skip aspects of the bottom-up, step-by-step process. Doing so risks a weak structure, which in turn risks the public collapse of your bridge under the pressure of audience scrutiny. Ouch!

You build a strategic story in seven steps. Each step answers a question:

1. "Where are we headed?" Here, "we" includes you and your audience. A clear picture of the better future will inspire them. In step one, you **envision the better future.**
2. "Where is the audience coming from?" To persuade people, you must first understand where they've been, what they have experienced, and how that might influence their thoughts and feelings about moving toward the better future. In step two, you **empathize with your audience.**
3. "How much can you ask of the audience?" Persuading people means that they experience a change in their perspective. Change is hard, in part, because it means both letting go of their current perspective as well as adopting a new one. Make that change as easy as possible. In step three, you **select an *achievable* new perspective.**
4. "What is your message?" Every strategic story raises a key question in the audience's minds. Your message is the short answer to that question. That message is supported by a set of arguments. In step four, you **develop your message and arguments.**
5. "How will you open and close?" Your opening must lead your audience into your message and supporting arguments.

It would be overly ambitious to go out on a first date with an engagement ring in your pocket.

It's equally naïve in business to expect instant approval for your ideas. Approaching the journey stage by stage is more likely to succeed, and it's often faster.

Your closing asks them to act. Success means engaging them into your arguments and requested action. In step five, you **create an engaging opening and closing.**

6. "What is the flow of the story?" The clarity and power of your story depends greatly on the sequence in which your audience receives your content. In step six, you **storyboard your communication.**
7. "How should you communicate with them?" The medium or media you chose should suit the context and content of the communication. Finally, in step seven, you **select and prepare appropriate media.**

The next section gives you an overview of each step so that you can build your own strategic stories. The seven-step process is summarized on pages 112–113.

The visually stunning Bixby Bridge in Big Sur, California opened in 1932 during the Great Depression. Although it cost little to build,[9] it demonstrates that a bridge can be both functional and beautiful. While our primary focus in this book is on function (clear, robust, persuasive stories), you can also give your audience a wonderful experience as they cross your bridge. We explore this in Cruxio's workshop, *"Persuasion Tactics."*

"Put [the truth] before them briefly so they will read it, clearly so they will appreciate it, picturesquely so they will remember it, and above all, accurately so they will be guided by its light."[10]

—Joseph Pulitzer

NEWSPAPER PUBLISHER AND FOUNDER OF THE PULITZER PRIZES

Envision the better future

Step 1

Align your bridge toward the better future

Empowering people with the means and authority to make decisions is useless unless they have a vivid picture of the destination.

Strategic stories change a business by either starting or continuing a journey toward a better future. As Figure 1 (page 30) illustrates, it's a multi-stage journey: the bridge you're building now—your current strategic story—is one of several bridges that your audience must cross to get there.

To inspire others to pursue this better future, do these two things:

1. Envision this future yourself
2. Communicate your vision

1. Envision this future yourself. By clearly envisioning the future in your own mind, you'll have the confidence to head in the right direction and effectively communicate your vision. Think of this in terms of strategy and tactics. Strategy describes your destination and therefore, direction. Tactics describe the near-term actions required to move in that direction. Your strategic story advocates the near-term actions needed to move your audience one stage

Identify your target audience

By persuading the right individuals or groups to cross your bridge, you can be confident that, over time, others will follow—even in business we are social creatures! For this reason, you need to determine *who* you're inviting to cross your bridge: this select group is your target audience.

Targeting is important because the broader the audience you try to persuade, the more dilute your message. The more dilute your message, the lower your chances of success. Conversely, the narrower your audience, the more you can tailor your message, concentrating its power and increasing your chances of success.

Business isn't democratic, and neither is strategic communication. Whether you're communicating to a thousand people or a dozen, some groups or individuals will have more influence than others. If you know whom to target and tailor your message to them, your chances of success will increase. While you don't want to alienate the rest of the audience, your primary focus will be on those whose support you need to move one stage closer to the better future. From here on, "audience" will mean *target audience*.

closer to the better future. If that future is clear in your mind's eye, you're more likely to advocate appropriate actions. Without that clarity, you risk heading in the wrong direction, which will frustrate your audience and diminish your credibility.

2. Effectively communicate your vision. Management guru Peter Drucker said, "The ultimate task of a leader is to create human energies and human vision."[11] But how do you create that vision so others will follow? Leaders struggle with this. "Vision Statements" are notoriously vague or generic; they mean different things to different people.

Vivid pictures enable the audience to imagine themselves living and working in this better future, offering them an appealing image of what will have changed compared with today, and why it needed to change. This kind of clarity helps people make appropriate near-term tactical decisions. Empowering people with the means and authority to make decisions is useless unless they have a vivid picture of the destination.

Here's the first sentence of a real vision statement from an early-stage drug discovery company:

> "Our Vision is to be recognized as a leading specialty biopharmaceutical company at the forefront of innovation for patients with unmet medical needs."

It's hard to *envision* what this recognition would look like, where it would come from, and by what measure it would be considered leading. This vague aspiration, couched as a vision statement, could apply to any emerging biopharmaceutical company, so it's neither differentiating nor particularly inspiring. Adding that they focus on patients with "unmet medical needs" makes them . . . a drug discovery company.

Platitudes don't enable the reader to envision anything.

Equip your audience with mental photos or videos of their future

Develop relevant, realistic scenes from the future that could be captured in a photo or video clip. This enables your audience to visualize themselves being in that future and to extrapolate, "If this is true, then these other things must also be true." For example, in the late 1970s, Bill Gates and Paul Allen repeated the ridiculous notion that there would be "a computer on every desk and in every home."[12] This mental "photograph from the future" suggested that the cost, size, and personal utility of computers would be drastically different from the massive mainframes of the 1970s.

"I believe that this nation should commit itself to . . . landing a man on the moon and returning him safely to the Earth."

John F. Kennedy, 1961

"I have a dream that one day . . . little black boys and black girls will be able to join hands with little white boys and white girls as sisters and brothers."

Dr. Martin Luther King, 1963

"Maybe this is what the future will look like: fresh, clean water will be so rare it will be guarded by armies. Water as the next oil—the next resource worth going to war over."

Anita Roddick, 2004

Figure 2: Powerful pictures from the future[13]

The two inspiring quotes from the early '60s are good examples of describing a better future. The quote from Anita Roddick, an environmental activist and founder of The Body Shop, illustrates the power of describing a worse future—the consequences of inaction—an idea that we will explore in the planned sequel to this book, *Bridge-Building Insights*.

These visionary pictures are not literal photos or videos—they can't be because the better future doesn't exist yet—they are primarily verbal descriptions that enable the audience to imagine what it looks and feels like to be in that future.* Custom illustrations can enrich these verbal descriptions in some cases, but stock photography can't help you here. The purpose behind creating mental photos or videos is to keep the imagery relevant and real. Offering these visuals for your audience also prevents the use of symbolic images such as the cliché of an arrow buried in a bullseye.

Consider describing a photo or video that invites your audience to envision the future during your opening. Say, for example,

*The exception is where the better future has been achieved elsewhere, in which case literal photos or videos of that achievement provide compelling examples that will support your message and reduce resistance.

Example 1

Continuous pharmaceutical manufacturing

Today, many medicines take more than twelve months to manufacture from start to finish. The process takes several steps, which often occurs in facilities located in different countries. An undetected quality issue in an early step may not be caught until tests are run on the finished product, resulting in the loss of multiple batches made over previous months.

Several pharma companies are progressing toward continuous manufacturing in which a drug is made in one facility, continuously (not in batches), with real-time quality testing. Production would be measured in hours, not months. The magnitude of the challenges—technical, regulatory, and logistic, to name a few—is matched only by the scale of the investment required. The following are examples of pictures from a better future in which continuous manufacturing is routine. The pictures are matched to business functions to illustrate how you can tailor pictures from the same future to different audiences.

Audience	Mental Photo or Video from the Future
Finance	In this future, we will no longer have the costs of large inventories, scrapped batches, and multiple plants in different countries. We will reduce the risk of investing in new capacity that turns out to be unnecessary, as often happens today. As a result, our annual report will reflect a 7% improvement in the use of operating assets [mental photo].
Sales and Marketing	In this future, it won't be any easier to predict the unit sales of a newly launched product, but we will be able to respond to unexpected demand within weeks, not months or years. We won't face the embarrassment of explaining stock-outs to customers [mental video] or the disappointment of missing our revenue targets.
Leadership	In this future, we will report a 7% improvement in the use of operating assets and be able to respond to demand changes within weeks. If we take the lead by acting now, everyone at this table will be in demand for interviews and speeches [mental video] in a few years' time because we will have pioneered an industry revolution!

"Imagine a future in which you . . ."—completing the sentence with a scenario that provides a clear, strong, and positive contrast with the pain points of the current situation. For example, in the US, one pain we all share is a maddeningly complex tax code. A pitch for simplifying tax filing could begin, "Imagine that five years from now you could sit at your home computer and file your taxes in fifteen minutes!" From this simple picture the audience can extrapolate that many things would be different in this future, starting with a simpler tax code, but likely also including greater online security, and the ability to present aggregated financial data through a well-designed interface that is neatly integrated with state and federal government systems.

We can dream, can't we?

"All of my best decisions in business and in life have been made with heart, intuition, guts . . . not analysis. If you can make a decision with analysis, you should do so. But it turns out in life that your most important decisions are always made with instinct, intuition, taste, heart."[14]

—Jeff Bezos

FOUNDER AND CEO, AMAZON

Step 2

Empathize with your audience

To build a solid bridge, engineers survey the environment of the crossing. They consider soil, rock, and seismic conditions, the bridge's on-ramp, the distance that can be effectively spanned, and the off-ramp. In this step of the process, you consider where the audience is and has been. You survey the on-ramp side of the bridge.

The intent of your survey is to empathize with your audience. How are they likely to be feeling at the moment you invite them to step onto your bridge? That will depend on what they expect of you, the content, and the experience. It also depends on factors beyond your communication—their broader environment intellectually, emotionally, and physically.

Empathy requires understanding. By understanding where they are now, and where they've been, you'll be able to assess how far they might be willing to go in the next stage of the journey. As we know from Kahneman's Nobel Prize-winning insights and much research since, that willingness is greatly influenced by emotions. With both understanding and empathy, you'll be better able to build strong relationships with your audience.

Explore your audience's backdrop

You'll recall from pages 12 and 18 that the word "Backdrop" engraved on the Cruxio Bridge model represents factors that may influence your audience's willingness to step onto your bridge. In the context of moving toward the better future, explore these backdrop issues to avoid being blindsided. Forewarned is forearmed!

The backdrop includes your audience's assumptions, preconceptions, biases, beliefs, and frame of reference—the lens through which they're predisposed to view your story. Backdrop issues may be *related* or *unrelated* to moving toward the better future.

Related backdrop issues. Look for issues that might be directly related to your communication. Familiarize yourself with baggage that may drag them down, such as past failures that could sour potential support. Anticipate real or imagined threats that your communication might pose to individuals or groups. Don't overlook the minefields of culture and politics!

These questions will help you explore your audience's related backdrop issues:

- Have there been past failures (related to this enterprise)?
- Are there initiatives that could be viewed as competing?
- Who might feel threatened or disrespected?

Unrelated backdrop issues. Broader factors can eclipse your message. Be realistic about your audience's priorities: what matters to you may not matter to them. A backdrop of budget cuts, crises, or other major initiatives might suggest your timing is off. It would be, um, "brave" to advocate for lavish investment during budget cuts, or to pitch for additional headcount amidst layoffs, for example. If you're new to an organization's culture, tread carefully and with guidance. Sometimes the "strategic" in strategic story means waiting for the right moment—and being ready to seize it!

Immediate factors can also get in the way. You're less likely to get support from an audience that's hungry, tired, worn down, running behind schedule, or eager to leave. By anticipating this kind of possibility, you'll have the 10-minute version of your story ready for your scheduled half-hour presentation.

Asking these kinds of questions will help you explore your audience's unrelated backdrop issues:

- What current factors could eclipse this communication?
- Could the timing of this communication be a problem?
- Does this communication conflict with the organization's culture?

Another useful way to consider backdrop issues is to assess whether they originate from *beliefs* or from *context.*

Beliefs. Your audience's beliefs (assumptions, preconceptions, biases, etc.) can be powerful barriers. Learn about your audience and put yourself in their shoes, both rationally and emotionally. Some beliefs are based on easily corrected knowledge gaps, but others—such as entrenched biases—run deeper. If you fail to factor in these beliefs, you'll risk trying to push your audience

Example 2

Removing a backdrop misconception to clear a path to the message

Recently, a drug discovery client sought funding to advance a promising breakthrough that could prevent infections by all influenza strains with a single dose in a flu season. If successful, their non-vaccine approach would be a true "universal" preventative offering significant advantages over current vaccines.

A backdrop issue was the common misconception that current seasonal vaccines work well. They don't. For example, the CDC estimates the 2019–2020 flu vaccine was 45% effective.[15] The funding pitch corrected this misconception during the opening, clearing the path to the scale of the unmet medical need and the corresponding investment opportunity.

further than they're willing to go. The result will not be pretty.

The audience's beliefs extend to trustworthiness and credibility. If trust or credibility are likely to be issues, you must address them before you can hope to progress. Ideally, you'd do so before the communication but if that's not possible, address them in your opening.

Context. Changes in the environment can work for or against you. Forces that create urgency are often positive. For example, consider recent events, competitive actions, or new requirements that might create a relevant sense of urgency for your audience. Conversely, environmental changes such as the budget cuts and competing priorities mentioned earlier can create barriers. Context also applies to the immediate environment such as a tired, hungry audience.

Explore your audience's current perspective

The backdrop is one of many factors that shape your audience's current perspective. The current perspective is marked on the road surface because that's what the audience experiences as they step onto the bridge. To explore their current perspective, you need to explore what *underlies* it. That's why on the Cruxio Bridge model, the roadbed directly beneath "Current Perspective" is engraved, "Thinking, Feeling, Doing." To understand their current perspective, ask "What is the audience likely to be *thinking, feeling,* and *doing* at the beginning of the communication?"

These kinds of questions will help you explore your audience's current perspective:

Thinking

- What knowledge gaps might they have?
- Who or what influences them (internally and externally)?
- What logic might cause them to resist change?

Feeling

- What fears might they have about crossing the bridge?
- What hopes might they achieve by crossing the bridge?
- Could they see themselves as special (e.g., exempt)?

Doing

- What reading might they have done?
- What conversations might they have had?
- What other actions might they have taken related to moving toward the better future?

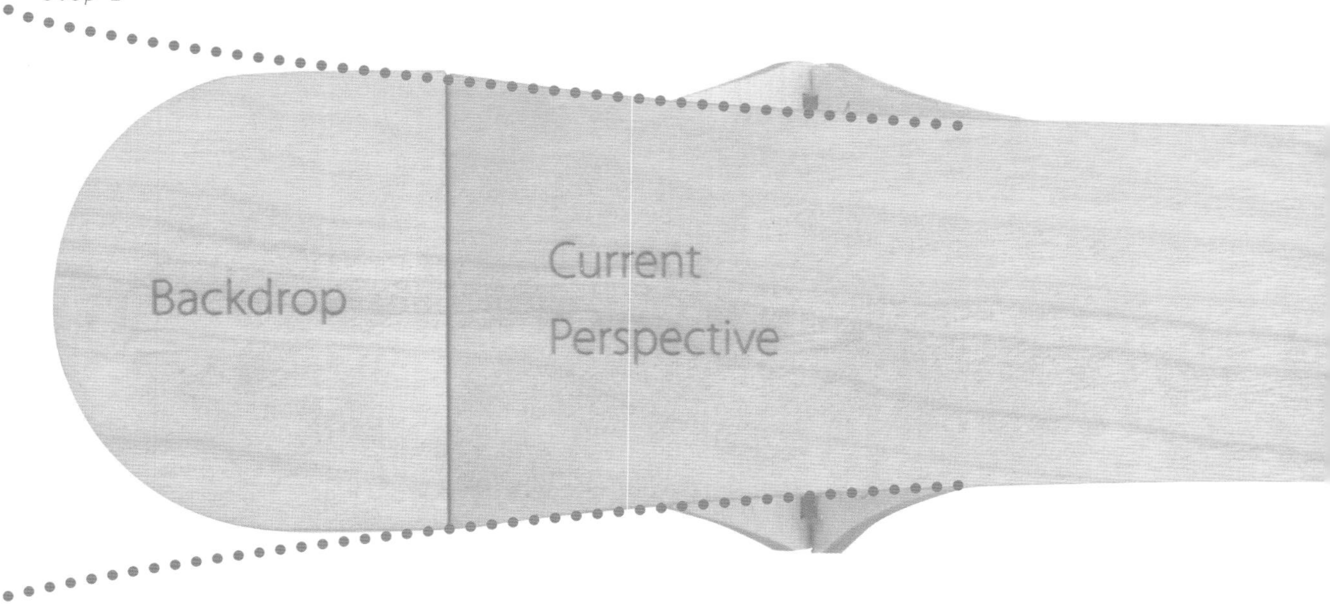

Backdrop

Current Perspective

You may have noticed that the bridge is wider at its entrance. This shape is a reminder that your audience's views are diverse. An effective strategic story will align their perspectives, which is why the bridge becomes narrower at its exit.

Thoroughly anticipate resistance

Understanding your audience's reasons to resist crossing your bridge is critically important in exploring the current perspective. Consider both the *nature* and the *degree* of resistance.

Nature. People tend to hide emotional resistance. For example, an executive may anticipate that your communication will threaten their power, control, or status. That executive is unlikely to voice such private fears directly, but they will certainly articulate resistance. This resistance will be presented as emphatic *rational* arguments . . . but have no doubt: the volatile fuel beneath their

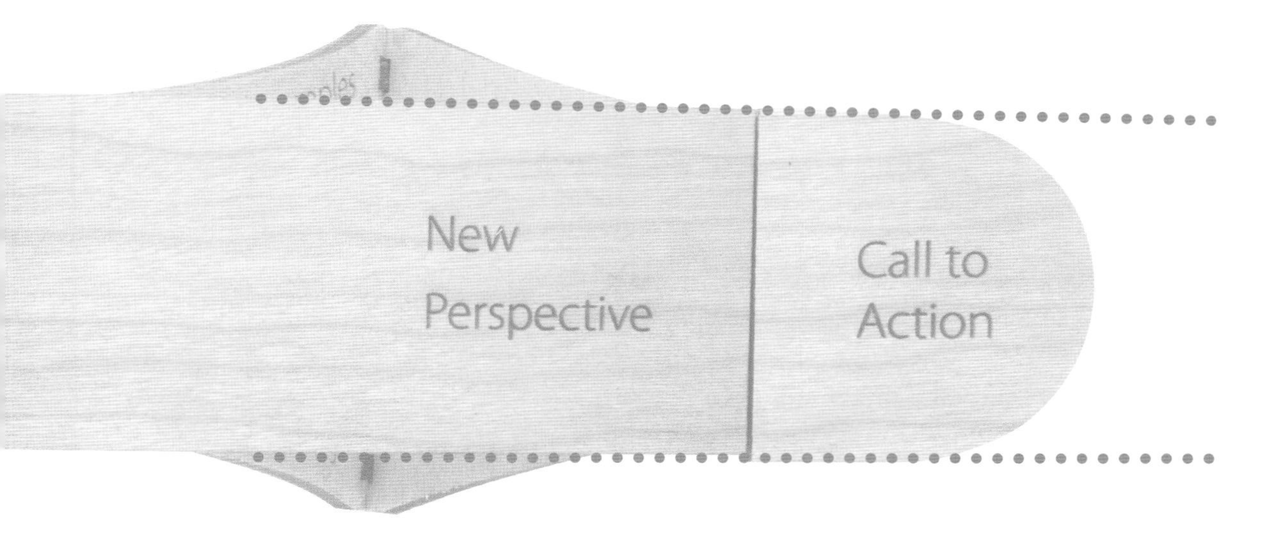

arguments is *emotional*. You can never win such arguments. Deeply personal resistance is like a ticking bomb: you must act in advance to defuse the emotion or to isolate the explosion so that it won't damage you and your chances of success.

Understanding your audience's reasons to resist is critically important in exploring the current perspective.

Degree. Your audience's resistance stems from their backdrop, their current perspective, and how much you ask them to do. The stronger the resistance, the smaller your request should be. It's okay to begin with a small request: you need to overcome inertia before building momentum.

To understand these factors, talk with audience representatives if you can. If that's not possible, talk to people who know them.

Understand how your audience sees you

Research shows that the more your audience trusts you, finds you credible, likes you, and sees you as being like them, the more likely they are to agree to act.[16,17]

Look toward the better future through your audience's eyes and ask how they see you as the advocate for change. These kinds of questions are a good starting point:

- How might they question your motives?
- How could you build trust and dispel suspicion?
- What could build your credibility in their eyes?
- What things could stand in the way of them liking you—and how could you change that in advance?
- What commonalities make you part of their tribe?

"Would you persuade, speak of Interest, not of Reason."[18]

—Benjamin Franklin
1734 *Poor Richard's Almanack*

Select an achievable new perspective

Step 3

How much can you ask of your audience?

In the previous step, you worked to understand where your audience had come from. Here, you think about where they're going—how far, specifically, you can reasonably ask them to move toward the better future. On the Cruxio Bridge model, the far riverbank is labeled "Call to Action." This is what you will ask your audience to do to enable the next stage of the journey. Their agreement to act requires a change in their perspective.

How much can you ask of your audience as they step off the bridge? Are your travelers fresh or weary? Hopeful or afraid? Eager or reluctant? You'll know the answer to these questions because of the work you did in step two to understand their current perspective—what they would likely be thinking, feeling, and doing as you invite them onto your bridge.

Your goal here is to tailor the length of the bridge to your audience.

In this step, you determine what you can realistically expect your audience to be thinking, feeling, and doing as they step off the bridge at the end of your communication. In the Cruxio process, we call this the *new perspective* you want them to adopt. This new perspective must be some version of:

Thinking: this makes sense and is worth the risk.
Feeling: hope or fear, or both.
Doing: agreeing to act on a reasonable request.

It doesn't matter how nicely you ask if you're asking for too much.

As Figure 3 illustrates, if the change from the audience's current perspective to the new perspective is too big for them, they won't cross your bridge, they won't respond to your call to action, and they won't embark on the next stage of the journey. Your goal here is to tailor the length of the bridge to your audience.

Figure 3: Consider your audience's current perspective in selecting your proposed new perspective

Make a reasonable request

Imagine this: you've just led a successful meeting. You ask your colleagues to put their chairs back in place while you clean the whiteboard for the folks who will be using the room next. They readily help, and it's done in a minute. If, instead, you had asked your colleagues to reset the room, clean the board, polish the table, and vacuum the floor, most would let you know that they'd love to help, but they're needed elsewhere.

Here's where strategy meets persuasion: in the first case, you made a reasonable request: please reset the chairs. In the second case, you asked for more than they were willing to give and were refused.

Determining how much an audience will give is a strategic call. It doesn't matter how nicely you ask if you're asking for too much. This is true whether you're resetting a meeting room or asking for tens of millions of dollars in investment.

Rewards must always exceed resistance

In Step 2, you considered how the audience might resist moving toward the better future. They will only cross your bridge if the rewards outweigh their resistance. "Rewards" encompass both the *hope of gain* and the *avoidance of pain.* Research shows that we are significantly more motivated to avoid a loss (a form of pain) than to gain something of equivalent value.[19,20] This suggests that avoidance of pain is a powerful motivator, so pay special attention to near-term rewards *(this* bridge) that could remove or reduce any of the audience's pain points.

"Rewards" encompass both the hope of gain *and the* avoidance of pain.

Figures 4A and 4B illustrate that

- Rewards must always exceed resistance.
- The more that rewards exceed resistance, the further your audience will be willing to go.

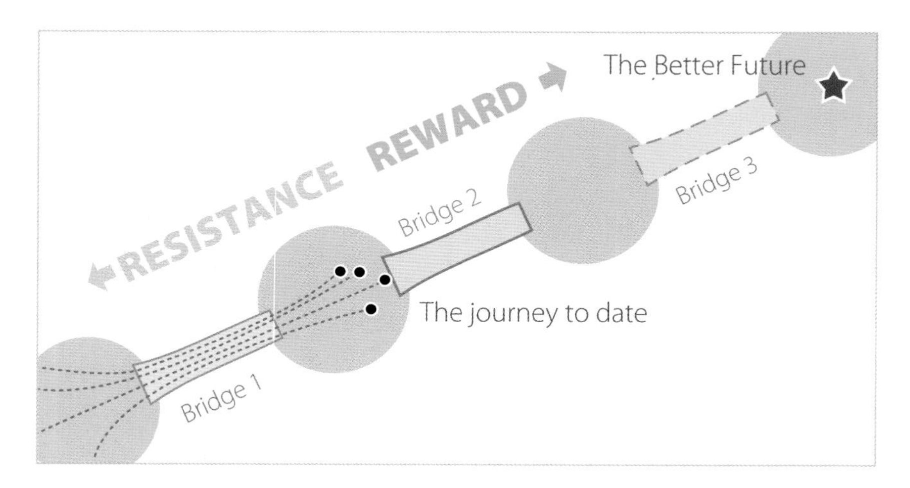

Figure 4A: Rewards must always exceed resistance

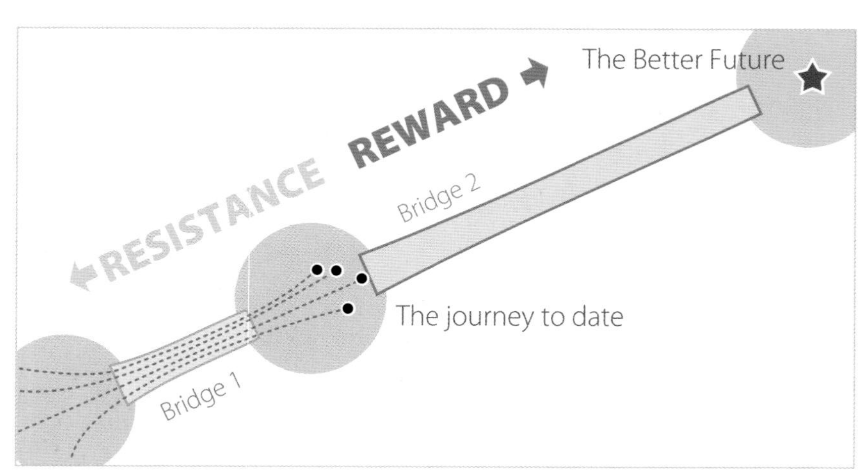

Figure 4B: With strong rewards, you can take the audience further

The trade-off between resistance and reward is difficult to fathom. To solve this complex human equation, we contrast their current perspective with a few "experimental" new perspectives.

Experiment iteratively to find a new perspective

Since the natural tendency is to overreach, experiment to find a practical new perspective. Here's a methodical way to get there:

1. Begin by reviewing the audience's current perspective.
2. Sketch out what you want the audience to be thinking, feeling, and doing at the end of this communication.
3. Note how the audience might resist.
4. Note the rewards you can offer the audience for crossing this bridge.
5. Ask yourself whether the rewards realistically exceed the resistance.
6. If not, try another experimental new perspective, or if you're struggling, return to step two and narrow your target audience.

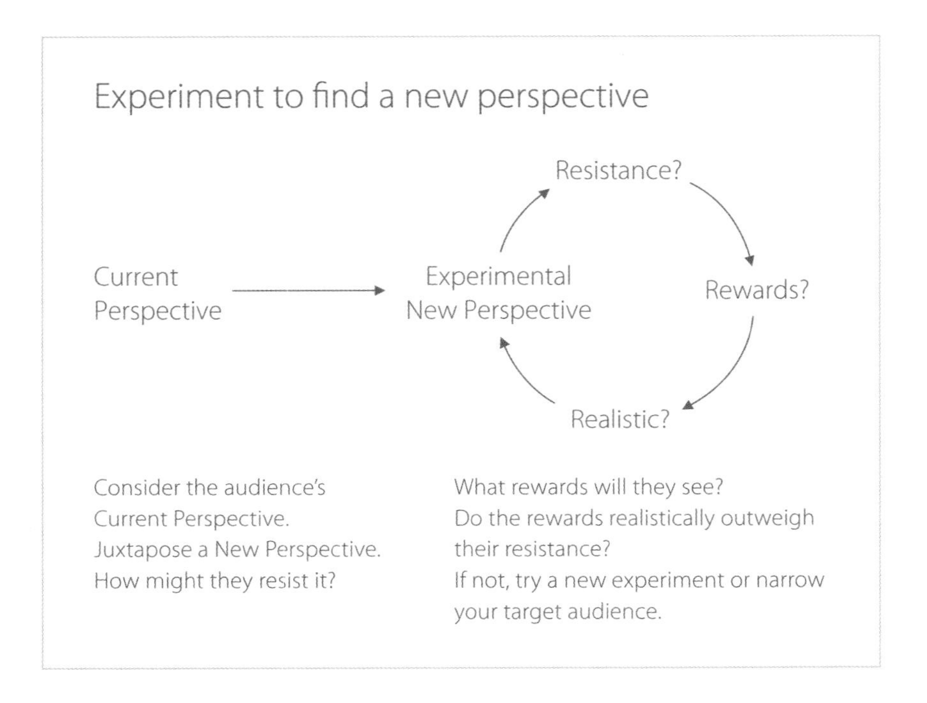

Figure 5: Experiment to find a new perspective

As you weigh the balance of resistance and rewards, you'll almost certainly end up asking for less than you want.

Really?!

Yep.

Why?

If you ask the audience to go further than they're willing, they'll say, "No!" Once anchored to a firm position, it will be more difficult to move them. Instead, by aiming for an achievable change in perspective and making a reasonable request, you make it easier for them to say, "Yes!"

Don't try to build a bridge to the moon. Achieving modest progress that yields near-term rewards will help you overcome inertia, build credibility, and destabilize naysayers. It will encourage those you lead and bolster the decision-makers who supported your first successful step. Better still, in most cases, taking a smaller step than you'd imagined won't slow you down.

Balance the audience's current perspective with what you could *realistically* expect them to be thinking, feeling, and doing at the end of your communication—your focus is *this* bridge. Find ways to dial up rewards or reduce resistance—by asking for less, for example. Feel highly confident that your audience will buy in. Factor in your call to action, which can be, in itself, a reason to resist. If you struggle to find a realistic new perspective, narrow your target audience so you can tailor their rewards more effectively.

Identify near-term, personal, and professional rewards

Near-term rewards. We're not good at delaying gratification, which is why it's important to link near-term rewards to the current call to action. Unless your audience can see net value in crossing your bridge, they're not going to do it. Even if they dearly want the better future, hoping for that distant dream won't compel action today.

Personal rewards. These satisfy intrinsic desires for things such as recognition, relationship, and power. You know they're powerful motivators, but people seldom acknowledge these deeply private desires—especially in business. In the business of persuasion though, we'd be missing out if we didn't consider them!

In Example 3, the Project Alpha decision-makers could see that success would reflect well on them. They probably didn't openly discuss that benefit, but did it play a role? Absolutely!

Since personal rewards address private needs, you can't address them directly. That's okay. You can raise them in your audience's minds without being explicit. For example, you could point to people just like them who succeeded by following a path similar to your proposal.[21] You can flip this to highlight failures that resulted from *not* following your proposed path—and implicitly, the ensuing career damage.

The more you can help your audience see personal rewards, the more likely they'll cross your bridge because people are highly motivated to serve their own interests. They won't talk about these powerful intrinsic motivations, but they will act on them! So, consider your target audience's personal rewards and look for ways to subtly convey them, as in this example:

> Our new CEO said she promoted Paul because he was an independent thinker who takes calculated risks. She's willing to back fresh, well-considered ideas but won't look favorably on any of us if we sit on our hands over this issue. While any new approach exposes us to some risk, we believe this proposal is likely to succeed and will position us well in the coming months."

Example 3

Project Alpha succeeded by offering near-term rewards

A clinical diagnostics manufacturing client made a pitch for a global IT project we'll call Alpha. It was an ambitious initiative that would require $20 million to complete over three years. As with most large-scale projects, Alpha was planned in stages, with pilots in Stage 1.

We had considered the decision-makers' backdrop and current perspective before experimenting with a new perspective that would support providing the $20 million required to fund the project. It was immediately obvious that the decision-makers would be reluctant to approve this level of funding. The project's failure could hurt the company and damage their reputations.

All was not lost! Success in the pilots would demonstrate the larger project's feasibility. Why not start there? Focusing on the pilots would require a much smaller change in perspective. We experimented with this near-term horizon in mind.

After this experiment the project leader was confident that, by the end of the strategic story, the decision-makers would *think* that funding the pilots was a good decision, *feel* comfortable supporting them, and *do* what was asked: approve a limited investment. So, instead of pitching for the whole $20 million, the project leader requested $2 million for the Stage 1 pilots.

The outcome? The decision-makers readily approved this relatively modest funding request because it diminished their personal and financial risks, and success would reflect well on them. If the pilots failed, they could position their support as a reasonable investment in innovation and learning. The pilots did succeed and, based on these successes, the following stages were funded.

This illustrates two types of personal reward. One is the hope of gaining the new CEO's favor, the other fits the "avoidance of pain" category: her disfavor if the group fails to act!

Figure 6: Self-interest is a powerful motivator

Professional rewards. In contrast, professional rewards that benefit the business are safe for discussion. Since decisions are usually justified in terms of value to the business, many communicators focus their efforts at this end of the spectrum, supported by volumes of data and logic. Often, those efforts are inexplicably frustrated. Why? Because they failed to consider motives originating from the deeply private end of the spectrum. When you hear a lot of talk but see no action, either there are emotional reasons to resist at play, or the personal rewards are too small or too distant to merit action. In many cases, it's not enough that a proposal is good for the business; people have to see what's in it for them. Figure 6 sums up this slightly cynical conclusion.

To get action, explore the length of the spectrum. You'll find personal rewards that overlap with professional rewards—for example, the leader of a business unit or function may think both in terms of "the business" (the company) and "my business" (the leader's area of responsibility). To get action, link personal rewards to business goals.

Presentation expert Nancy Duarte estimates that a one-hour, 30-slide presentation takes between 36 and 90 hours to prepare.[22] However long it takes you, allocate a generous portion of that time to strategically important aspects such as knowing where you want to go, understanding and empathizing with your audience, and determining how much they might be willing to change their perspective.

The new perspective determines the length of your bridge

By assessing how far your audience will move in this stage of the journey, you determine the length of this bridge. In Step 2, you assessed the audience's current perspective—what they were likely to be thinking, feeling, and doing. This is their starting point. In this step, you've determined the landing point for this bridge: the new perspective—what you want them to be thinking, feeling, and doing. Now that you've determined these two points, you can derive the message required to move your audience from one perspective to the other. That's why, in the Cruxio process, you determine your message and arguments *after* you've determined the new perspective. Doing so saves you from pursuing unrealistic paths and focuses your creative energy on achievable goals.

"All I know for sure is that the brain doesn't pay attention to boring things, and I am as sick of boring presentations as you are."

—Dr. John Medina

DEVELOPMENTAL MOLECULAR BIOLOGIST AND AUTHOR OF *BRAIN RULES*[23]

Develop your message and arguments

Step 4

The load-bearing arches of the Cruxio Bridge were inspired by Leonardo da Vinci's ingenious design of a single-span, stone-arched bridge held by friction and gravity. You don't have to be an engineer to appreciate the structural simplicity of his design compared with today's truss bridges, for example. Strategic stories follow a clear, simple structure based on da Vinci's bridge because business audiences want clarity, not complexity.

You'll recall that in every strategic story you raise one key question in your audience's minds.[*, 24] *One* question keeps things simple; it gives the story a clear focus. Choosing an effective question requires thought and experimentation, effort that your audience deserves if you expect to persuade them. The answer to that key, pivotal question is your message. It leads to the new perspective

The simplicity of Norway's interpretation of da Vinci's design (left) stands in stark contrast to today's truss bridges (above).

*Step four of the Cruxio process takes a leaf from the manual of major consulting companies like McKinsey and the Boston Consulting Group. They're in the business of answering their clients' most difficult questions. Their answers are invariably supported by a robust set of arguments based on Barbara Minto's Pyramid Principle. We apply aspects of this approach to every strategic story; in particular, the use of a key question and the pyramid form of arguments that support the message.

you want the audience to adopt. As Figure 7 illustrates, you'll communicate your message during your opening to frame your upcoming arguments, and then reprise it in closing. The essence of your message is the same in both cases, but it comes across differently to the audience. During your opening, it is seen as a proposal or a statement of your position because it hasn't been supported by arguments. In closing, you've presented the arguments and the message has been absorbed, so now the message seems to be a logical conclusion.

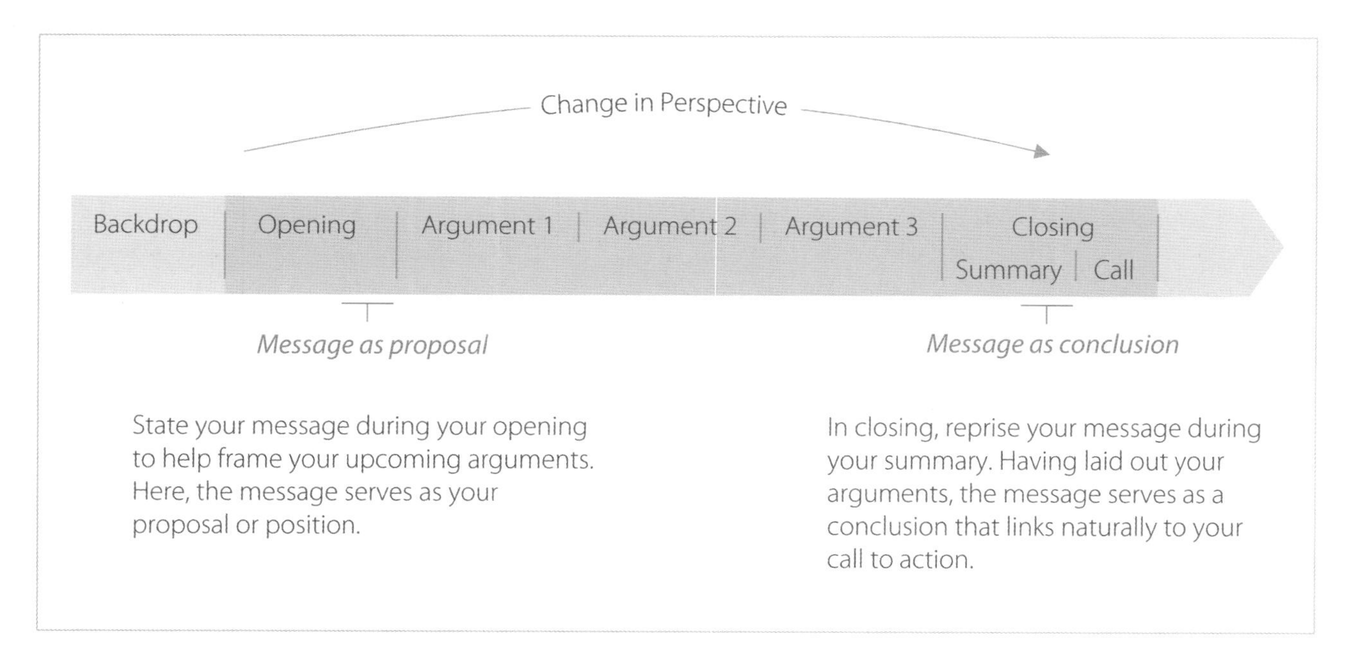

Figure 7: Your message, supported by arguments, changes your audience's perspective

Communicate a message, not a topic

"A message . . . conveys the so what, *whereas information merely conveys the* what."

—Jean-luc Doumont

What's the difference between a message and a topic? It becomes clear once you see it. Below are four examples of topics that have been translated into messages. In each case, the communicator tailors the message to the audience. The supporting arguments are shown in parentheses:

Topic	Message
A possible asset acquisition.	**Head of business development to the CEO:** "We recommend acquiring this asset because it will strengthen our portfolio and competitive position while reducing our costs." (Arguments demonstrate how the asset would strengthen the business in these specific ways.)
Process and equipment standardization.	**Global head of manufacturing to production site leaders:** "We'll increase productivity while improving quality and job satisfaction by standardizing core processes and equipment across all sites." (Arguments illustrate how standardization will deliver these benefits.)
Investing in a start-up company.	**Start-up CEO to potential investor:** "We would like to engage with you because we think we may fit your portfolio well." (Arguments reveal how the start-up may be a good fit for the investor's portfolio.)
A new cancer drug.	**Keynote speaker to fellow oncologists:** "I believe it's worth trying this new drug because it has advantages over the current standard of care." (Arguments show specific advantages.)

The value of a message is summed up beautifully by communication expert Dr. Jean-luc Doumont: "A message . . . conveys the *so what* whereas information merely conveys the *what*."[25]

Each of these messages conveys two meaningful elements:

1. The communicator's position.
2. Why their message matters—or should matter—to the audience.

By stating your position, you take a stand that crossing this bridge is important. In business, your message often includes a recommendation or proposal. When you use a phrase such as, "We recommend that . . . " or "We propose . . . " you combine your position with your proposal.

There are three phases in developing your story's message and supporting arguments. The first phase diverges to create options. The second phase converges to develop and refine the strongest option. In the third phase, you develop your message.

Phase 1: Explore key questions and supporting arguments

This divergent phase rapidly explores different sets of key questions and supporting arguments, only one of which will become the basis of your strategic story. Approach this phase with a creative, playful mindset.

Start by listing several key questions that, if raised in the audience's minds, would move them to the new perspective you want them to adopt. Select one question and follow these two steps to create a set of arguments:

1. Find two to four arguments that answer the question (see Figure 8).*
2. Apply two tests:

   - Does each argument directly answer the question?
   - Is each argument independent of the others?

If the argument set fails these tests you can:

- Adjust the arguments.
- Adjust the question.
- Try a different question.

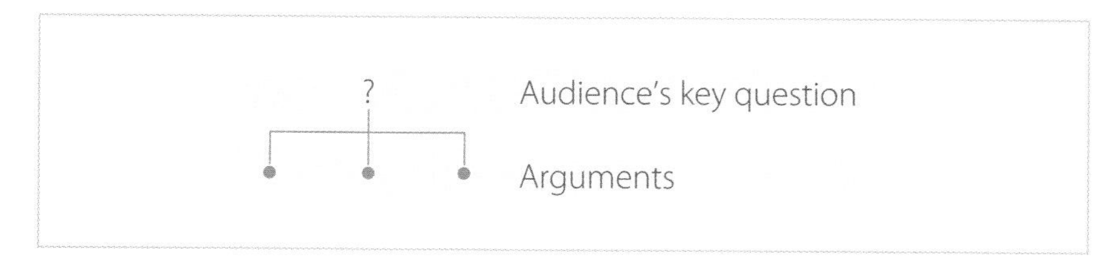

Figure 8: Phase 1: Diverge by creating different question-and-argument sets

When an outline passes these tests, don't stop! Continue to experiment with additional question-and-argument sets until you have generated three sets that pass both tests.

---

*In most cases, three independent arguments are all you need to answer a key question. Sometimes two are enough; occasionally four are needed. The advantage of ***in***dependent arguments is that if one is rejected but the others stand, you're still likely to succeed. Translated to the Cruxio Bridge model: if one arch fails, the remaining arches can support the road above. In contrast, ***inter***dependent arguments are complex and, like a weak link in a chain or a rusted load-bearing truss in a bridge, the failure of one can bring the whole thing crashing down.

Phase 2: Finalize your key question and supporting arguments

The intent in this phase is to converge on the most effective key question and set of answering arguments.

Review the three Phase 1 outlines through your audience's eyes, asking yourself which elements are most likely to persuade them to adopt your proposed new perspective. Sometimes one question-and-argument set stands clearly above the others. More often, you'll see promising ideas in different argument sets. In this more common situation, you can experiment by working "downward" from the question, or "upward" from a set of promising arguments. To work downward, select or adjust a promising question, then create or reuse existing arguments to answer it. To work upward, select a few promising arguments that seem to fit together, and find a key question that unites them.

Sketching high-level support for each argument, as shown in Figure 9, makes it easier to select your final candidate.

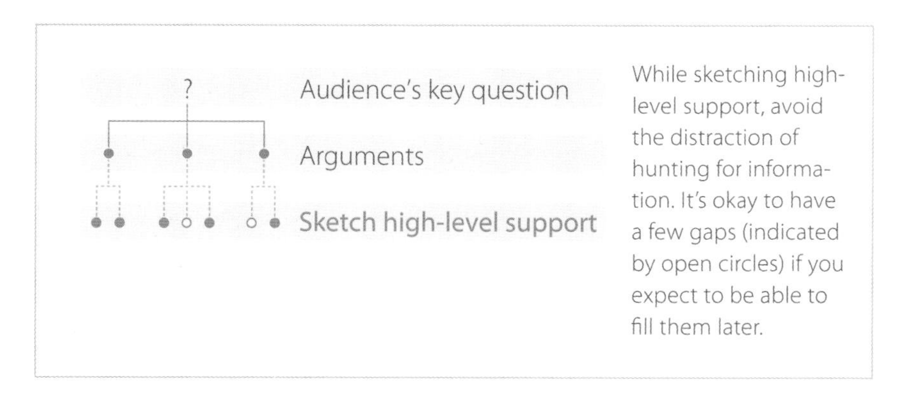

Figure 9: Phase 2: Converge on one question-and-argument set, sketching support for each argument

Once you've selected your final question-and-argument set, complete and refine the high-level support for each argument, as shown in Figure 10. Avoid getting bogged down in detail, but do ensure that the high-level support is, or will be, available.

Each argument is supported by a mix of some or all of these elements:

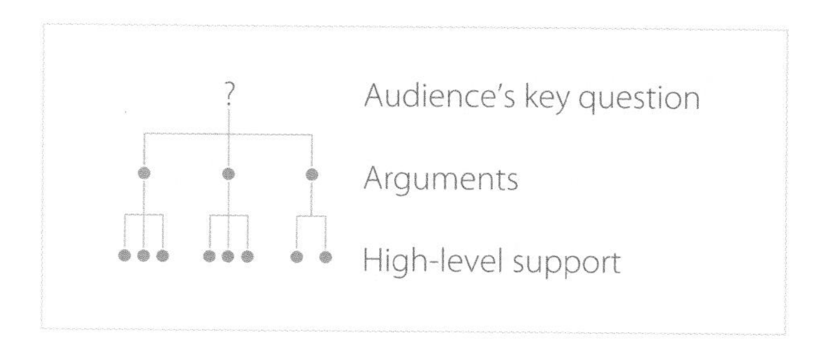

Figure 10: Complete and refine high-level support for each argument

- Data
- Facts
- Logic
- Examples

Data. Credible quantitative evidence can be highly persuasive *if* it conveys a message. Raw data is simply information; your job is to give it meaning. Solid, message-driven data reduces doubt, increases trust, and bolsters your argument—that's a powerful package! Providing a reputable citation will amplify that effect. Quantities engage the rational mind but they also speak to the emotional mind, which weighs the data's credibility . . . and yours.

Facts. The points about data apply equally to facts, and for the same reasons they appeal both rationally and emotionally. However, facts are not necessarily quantitative. Relevant, verified facts are a powerful tool in your persuasion arsenal.

Logic. It's easy to follow simple logical connections along the lines of "this, therefore that" but following more complex arguments takes concentration. If some in your audience miss, or do not believe, part of a deductive logical argument, they may not accept your conclusion. If the logic is complex or weak, or the audience is tired, they're likely to tune out and miss the point. Logic can be a valuable tool when it's uncomplicated and clear. As with data and facts, a well-made logical argument yields both rational and emotional support.

Examples. This broad category of support is rich with opportunity! Examples can include elements such as case studies, comparisons, photos, videos, props, and narratives. Examples operate differently from data, facts, and logic: they readily enable you to draw on human senses (e.g., sight, hearing, touch). As we've noted, people are more open to persuasion when they engage their senses.[26]

Example 4

Supporting an argument with data, facts, logic, and examples

A business leader is developing a set of arguments based on the key audience question, "How should we respond to our major competitor's sudden product recall?" The answering arguments support a message that advocates changes in manufacturing, marketing, and distribution. This example focuses on the first argument: manufacturing.

Although the year-to-date sales data do not yet indicate an increase in demand, the first arch of this bridge argues that the company should immediately start the process of adding another production shift. The leader has ready access to the data, facts, logic, and examples shown in Figure 11.

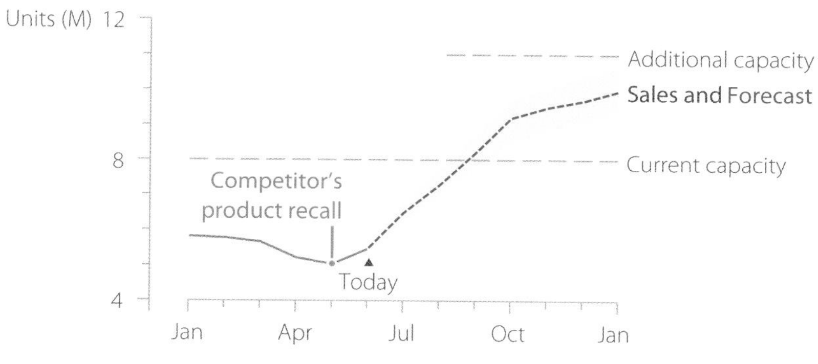

Facts

- Year-to-date sales of Product X that were in decline increased last month (June).
- Our major competitor recalled its product in May and industry analysts do not expect it to be able to supply for 12–18 months.
- Our current maximum production capacity is 8 million units per month.
- Internal analysis forecasts an increase ranging between 9 and 11 million units by January.
- By adding shifts, we can increase our maximum monthly capacity to 11 million units per month.
- It takes two months to add a shift.

Logic

- Demand for Product X is likely to increase because we are one of only three suppliers in this market, and because similar demand spikes have happened twice before.
- Since it takes two months to add a shift, if we don't start now, we won't be able to meet the full demand.

Examples

1. Five years ago, when we had to recall Product X, both of our competitors experienced demand spikes. Our major competitor's unit sales nearly doubled over eight months.
2. Three years ago, when our major competitor's supply was disrupted by a component shortage, Product X unit sales increased by 68% over six months. In that case, we delayed adding a shift and were unable to fully meet the industry's demand. Our smaller competitor happily filled that gap!

Figure 11: Support arguments with a mix of data, facts, logic, and examples

Examples that your audience can relate to personally will be more memorable and more likely to stimulate action.[27,28] While data and facts can pack a powerful punch, mixing them with effective examples will substantially increase your chances of success.

The resulting sketch of this argument is shown in Figure 12.

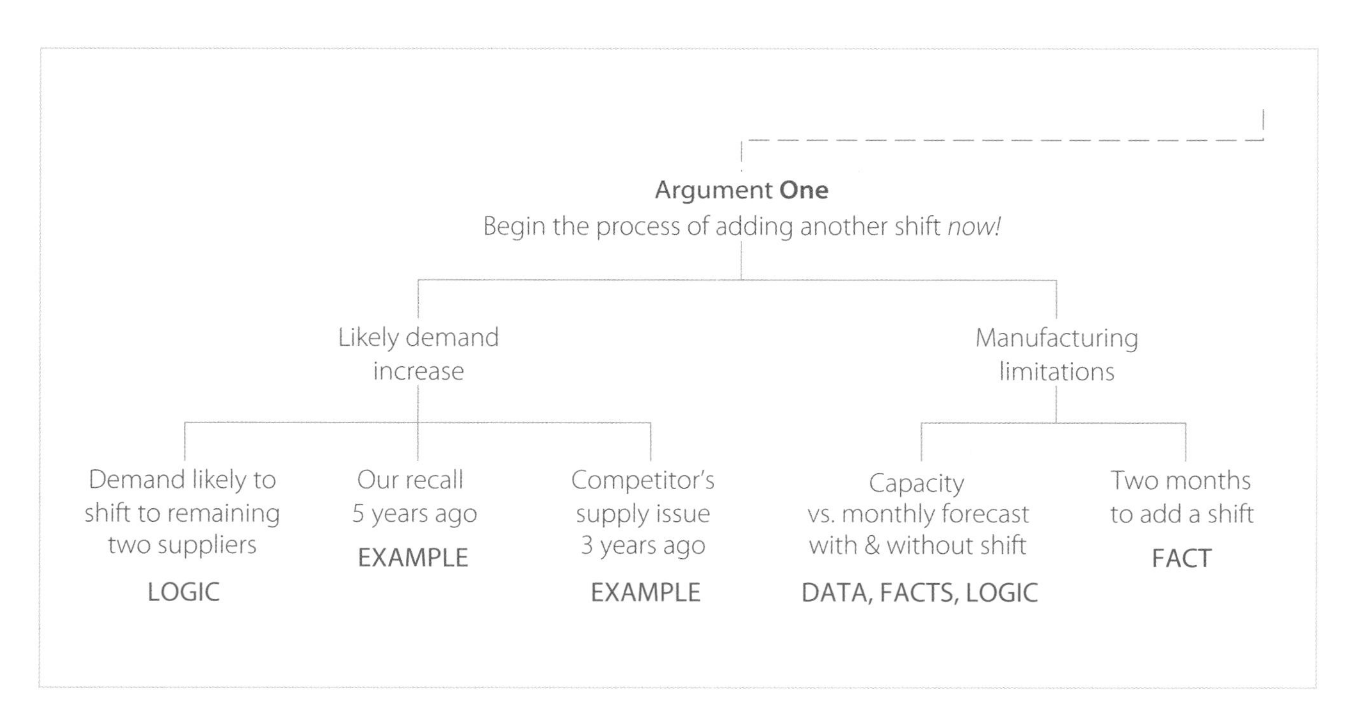

Figure 12: The business leader's convergent sketch of the manufacturing argument

As you can see, the argument boils down to two simple ideas supported by data, facts, logic, and examples.

1. Demand is likely to rise.
2. We won't be able to meet demand unless we add a shift, starting now.

Phase 3: Develop your message

In Phase 2, you selected one question-and-argument set. In this third phase, you convert that to a *message*-and-argument outline. Since a message summarizes the arguments, it serves as a summary answer. As such, it can be inserted between the audience's question and the arguments, as Figure 13 shows. This is useful because you'll always state your message, but in many cases, there's no need to raise the audience's key question explicitly—it remains implicit.

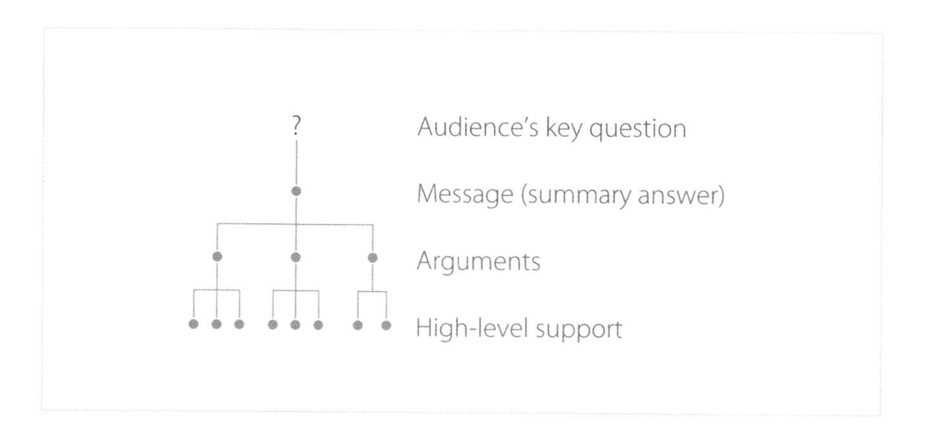

Figure 13: Phase 3: Develop your final message-and-argument outline

The message can either list the arguments or summarize them. Your choice of approach will depend on your story. Fortunately, it's an easy judgment call: simply say each version out loud. You'll hear which form is more likely to resonate with your audience. Let's apply these two approaches to the example of the keynote speaker on page 71.

Listing the arguments explicitly could sound like this: “I believe it’s worth trying this new drug because it offers greater safety, efficacy, and convenience over the current standard of care.”

Here’s the alternative summary form: “I believe it’s worth trying this new drug because it has advantages over the current standard of care.”

Oh! Having heard these two versions out loud you’ll hear another possibility: sometimes the two forms can be used together. The oncologist could lead with the summary form, which raises a little intrigue (tension!). It begs the question, “What advantages?” Following with the list of particular advantages releases that tension and frames the upcoming three arguments that cover safety, efficacy, and convenience. Here’s an example of that combination: “I believe it’s worth trying this new drug because it has advantages over the current standard of care: it’s safer, more effective, and more convenient for both patients and providers.”

Example 5

The message-and-argument outline for considering an acquisition

On page 71, you read the example of a message that a head of business development delivered to the CEO. Here is the message-and-argument outline of that strategic story. You can see that the arguments are independent by considering their underlying concepts. For each of the three arguments, the corresponding concepts are:

1. Portfolio strategy
2. Competitive position
3. Cost

*Each argument's higher-level concept is shown in blue.

"The more you leave out, the more you highlight what you leave in."[29]

—Henry Green
Novelist

Step 5

Create an engaging opening and closing

The three objectives of your opening

The backdrop is engraved on the left riverbank to remind you to consider issues that may influence your audience's willingness to step onto your bridge. Address negative backdrop issues in your opening because the audience *will* shut down if they feel that they've been dragged into a presentation of your interests, blithely ignoring their concerns or objections. Don't risk damaging their trust and your reputation.

Your opening should clear an inviting path to your message and its supporting arguments. To do this effectively, you need to hook your audience's rational and emotional minds. As in fishing, different fish require different hooks. Your work to understand and empathize with your audience in Step 2 becomes vital. What engages the hearts and minds of the board of directors probably won't do the same for an all-employee town hall meeting.

Your goal here is to sketch your opening and closing at a high level, so maintain the playful, creative mindset of the previous step. You'll get specific about execution in Step 6.

Your opening has three objectives, which are engraved on the bridge's foundation:

1. *Engage* the audience.
2. *Connect* with them personally.
3. *Frame* your upcoming arguments.

1. Engage. Seize attention from the outset. Your opening should end conversations and get your audience off their smart phones. Businesspeople want you to get to the point quickly. If your opening suggests you'll get to the point later, they're likely to tune you out until, hopefully, things get more interesting. Their behavior is based on experience: many presenters waffle at the beginning. Time-pressured businesspeople would rather read another email or send another text than waste time listening to a rambling introduction.

2. Connect. A powerful opening will start to build trusting relationships with the audience. Connect personally, because the more they see you as being one of them or like them, the more likely they will be open to you, your message, and your call to action.

3. Frame. Use your opening to raise the key question in your audience's minds. Raising the question helps to frame your answering message and its supporting arguments.

Figure 14 outlines the essential elements of your opening.

OPENING

Seize attention and direct it toward your message. Build relationships. Address negative backdrop issues. Consider including rewards and/or the better future.	Raise the key question in your audience's minds, then answer it by stating your message and topline arguments.
Seize attention and build relationships to open people to…	*…your message and arguments.*

Figure 14: Opening essentials

Seize the moment with your opening!

Your audience has expectations. Before you begin to speak—or they begin to read, if your communication is in print—they have a sense of anticipation (tension!): what's coming next? You can build on this . . . or blow it.

What do you want your audience to feel in that moment? Interested? Curious? Intrigued? Surprised? Shocked?! Many speakers waste this moment with formalities: extended greetings, thanks, introductions, and acknowledgments. Should you dispense with formalities? Not necessarily, but don't open with them. First, engage your audience's minds and hearts. If you are the host, a brief greeting and word of welcome is appropriate. If you are a guest speaker, have someone else introduce you to succinctly establish your credibility. Then get on with it, as in this example.

Example 6

A keynote speaker at an oncology conference

"Good morning! Thank you for your kind introduction, Judith."—pause—"The harsh reality for every oncologist in this room is that ultimately, we have to deliver bad news to three in ten patients who present with stage 3A colorectal cancer."

If you're an oncologist in that room—the target audience—those words will resonate personally and create anticipation. The opening engages intellectually and emotionally.

The speaker has been introduced and credentialed, so there's no need to start with a verbal résumé. Similarly, thanks and acknowledgements can be integrated into the talk. Acknowledgments in the moment make the credit more relevant: "Dr. Judith Rose's research gave us this valuable clinical insight . . . " This approach also avoids squeezing acknowledgments into the end of a talk. A list of credits isn't the last thing you want to leave with your audience, and under time pressure, that list is likely to sound rushed and perfunctory anyway.

Don't squander your golden opening opportunity. Embrace the audience, fuel their anticipation, and whisk them away!

The two objectives of your closing

The purpose of your strategic story is to move your audience to the new perspective so they will act. Consequently, your closing's objectives are to:

- Solidify the change in perspective.
- Translate it into action.

Solidify the change in perspective. By the end of your presentation, the audience has heard your arguments sequentially. They're not going to retain and connect them all; that's your job. The word "Summary" is engraved on the right side of the Cruxio Bridge to remind you to tie your persuasive package together.

Imagine that you've just finished your final argument and are about to transition to your closing, as shown in Figure 15.

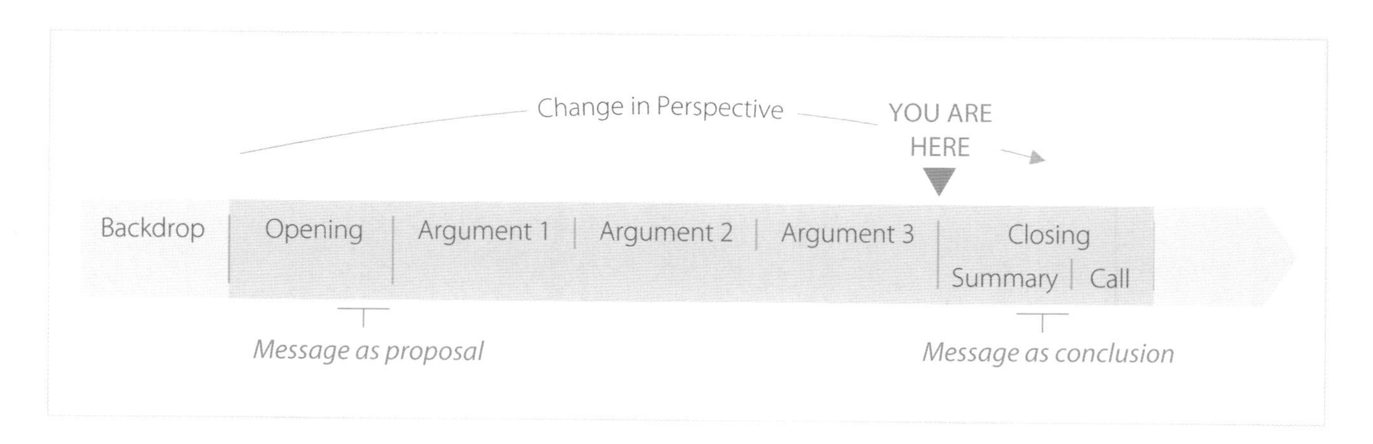

Figure 15: To develop your closing, reflect on your audience's experience

Let's pause here to reflect on your audience's experience to this point. You may recall that a business audience has three questions:

1. Why should I care?
2. Why should I believe you?
3. What do you want me to do?

Figure 16 maps these questions along the strategic story structure. Your opening answers the first question. The audience has let go of any backdrop issues that would have been a barrier. Your opening seized their attention and engaged them, in part by raising a key question in their minds. You stated your message, which gave your high-level answer to that question. In doing so, you outlined your position and showed the audience why they should care about your message. You also introduced the arguments that would support your message.

You made your first argument. At the end of that argument, the audience saw things in a different light. The same happened as you made your second and third arguments. Their experience to this point has been a series of responses to the opening and to each argument, as Figure 16 illustrates:

Opening: "I see why I should care about this!"
Argument 1: "I see things differently."
Argument 2: "I see things differently."
Argument 3: "I see things differently."

As you finish this third argument and transition to your closing—the point at which we have paused—your audience knows why they should care and sees things in a different light. Many will have already adopted the new perspective, others will be close to doing so.

Your summary reinforces why your audience should care and why they should believe you. In summarizing, reiterate your message and remind your audience of its high-level supporting

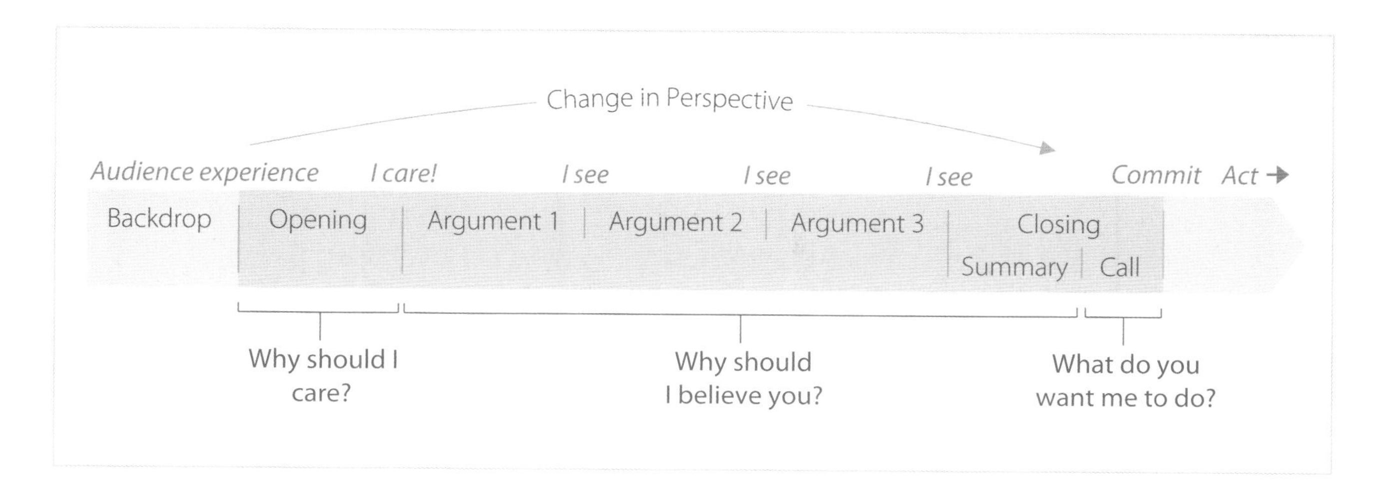

Figure 16: A strategic story addresses why an audience should care, believe, and act

arguments. The audience will hear your message as a conclusion now that they have absorbed the arguments in full. Remind your audience of the rewards they will receive by adopting the new perspective and acting on it. It's often persuasive to reprise one or two pictures from the better future here. The combination of rewards for crossing this bridge must outweigh their reasons to resist, so it's important that they embrace the complete package with their minds and hearts. Otherwise, they won't respond to your call to action.

Translate it into action. With the summary fresh in their minds, it's time to answer the question, "What do you want me to do?"

Ask the audience to act.

Be realistic about *how much* you can ask them to do and be specific about *what* you want them to do. They will act only if they see value to themselves personally and view the request as reasonable.

"People act on what they remember, not on what they forget."

—Dr. Carmen Simon

Sometimes it's practical to have a fallback option for your call to action. This fallback enables progress if your audience's reaction isn't as supportive as you had expected.

"People act on what they remember, not on what they forget."[30] That practical wisdom from Dr. Carmen Simon is a reminder to close memorably, encouraging people to follow your call to action. The "peak-end" rule[31] says, as its name suggests, we tend to judge an experience based on how we felt at its peak and its end . . . so, how you close matters!

Figure 17 provides a high-level guide to help you identify the essential elements of your closing.

CLOSING

Remind the audience why they should care. Show the combined strength of your arguments.

Remind the audience of their rewards for crossing this bridge. Optional: reprise the better future.

State your message as a conclusion and make a reasonable request for action.

Your summary reinforces the new perspective…

…and asks the audience to act!

Figure 17: Closing essentials

“Make sure you have finished speaking before your audience has finished listening.”[32]

—Dorothy Sarnoff

OPERA SINGER

Storyboard your communication

Step 6

Build a smooth, elegant bridge

In the previous two steps you outlined these structural elements: the opening, arguments, and closing. Now it's time to determine the *specific information* the audience will receive, and the *sequence* in which they'll receive it within each of these structures. Your choice of information and sequence greatly affects the audience's moment-to-moment experience, which influences their decision to cross your bridge. Storyboarding smooths out bumps that could distract your audience or weaken their confidence in the bridge and its designer . . . you! This step also helps avoid adding unnecessary material. Your audience wants enough but no more: provide them with a smooth road surface as they cross your bridge.

Give your audience the experience of a beautifully smooth road surface by thoughtfully selecting and sequencing information.

Tailor the sequence of arguments to your audience

To illustrate the importance of sequence, let's return to the example of the oncology speaker's keynote presentation about a new drug for treating stage 3A colorectal cancer (page 88). The speaker's message is, "I believe it's worth trying this new drug because it has advantages over the current standard of care." The supporting arguments outline three advantages: greater safety, improved efficacy, and more convenience.

In Figure 18, Sequence A presents these arguments following the normal course of drug development where safety comes first. Leading with "more convenience" as shown in Sequence B would frustrate an audience of oncologists, who would regard convenience as peripheral until they were assured the drug was safe and effective. If the audience were investors and the standout feature of the drug was improved efficacy, then leading with that argument would make sense.

Figure 18: Tailor the sequence of arguments to your audience

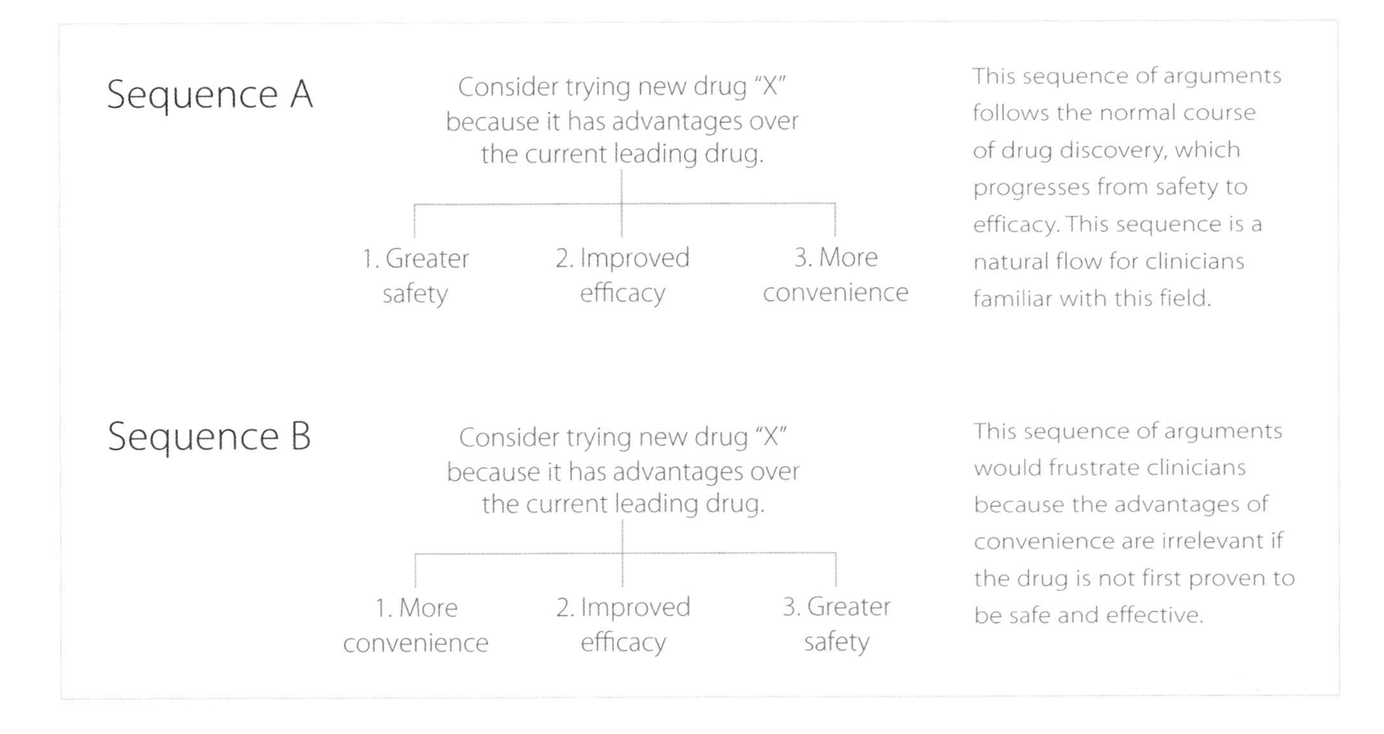

Plan your audience's moment-to-moment experience

There may be no "right" shape for your particular story, but there is a wrong shape: a flat line.

An engaging story has a shape. Writers refer to it as the story's arc. This shape reflects the ups and downs that the characters—and we—experience along their journey. While arc is mostly applied to the overall story's shape, it's also relevant to acts and scenes, and from one moment to the next.

Similarly, shape is relevant to your strategic story at every level. There may be no "right" shape for your particular story, but there is a wrong shape: a flat line. "Flat" is the dreary stream of data and facts spilling in a monotone from a presenter's lips. If you could bottle it, you'd have a blockbuster sleeping potion!

Yes, your strategic story must be rock solid—well supported by robust data, facts, logic, and examples—but it must be interesting, too.

What makes a story interesting? Dynamics. Moments of change. Moments where, for example, we experience conflict, contrast, challenge, anticipation, intrigue, tension, relief, surprise, realization, insight, humor, hope, or fear. Moments that prompt the audience to imagine something or to draw on their own experience, can be especially powerful. To create an interesting story, plan your audience's moment-to-moment experience.

Here are five ways that you can create an engaging, dynamic experience for your audience:

1. Create and release tension.
2. Offer stark contrasts.
3. Inject concrete elements.
4. Provide examples.
5. Spice with surprise.

1. Create and release tension. We are, by nature, curious. How could you pique your audience's curiosity? Compare "Here is the clinical study design . . . " with "To succeed, our study had to achieve two unprecedented clinical endpoints . . . ." The former *tells*. The latter *intrigues*: "Oh? What endpoints? Why? Was it successful?" Raising an implicit question creates a little tension ("What's coming next?"). Then you release that tension by revealing the answer.

2. Offer stark contrasts. Contrasts engage people. Today vs. tomorrow. Big vs. small. Fast vs. slow. Pricy vs. cheap. Look for opportunities to juxtapose elements. Nancy Duarte's thoughtful analysis of famous inspirational speeches reveals a pattern of contrasting "what is" (the present) with "what could be" (the better future).[33]

3. Inject concrete elements. Things that we perceive with our senses are concrete; those we cannot are ideas or concepts. Your message will stick better if you engage your audience's senses—through their imaginations or even literally—along with ideas and concepts.

4. Provide examples. A good example helps your audience envision application in their own world. Done well, it delivers relevance and evidence packaged as an engaging story that speaks to hearts and minds. What's not to love?

5. Spice with surprise. Surprise catches people both intellectually and emotionally. In a 2015 study of the most popular SlideShares, surprise was the single most reliable predictor that viewers would act by, for example, liking, sharing, or downloading a presentation.[34] Surprise is a spice. Like nutmeg, a little goes a long way.

Break patterns to distinguish key points

A steady stream of sameness is boring; nothing stands out. Distinctiveness influences what people understand and remember, so use distinctive elements to highlight your vital take-home points. You can overdo it, though—too many points of distinction will compete, so nothing will stand out. As a result, you will have little influence over which elements people remember. These facts suggest a balance: offer a predictable pattern, and then break the pattern to distinguish key points. By repeating your key points distinctively, they are more likely to stick in the minds of your audience.

To achieve a finessed balance, play with ideas out loud. This visceral exercise will give you a good sense of what your audience will experience. Go with your gut. Research shows that we prefer the familiar and predictable, but to confound things, it also shows that too much predictability is boring.[35]

We are complex beings.

"Naturally sticky ideas are stuffed full of concrete words and images."[36]

—Chip Heath and Dan Heath
Authors of *Made to Stick*

Select and prepare appropriate media

Step 7

If you will be communicating in person, your primary medium is . . . you! Your role is that of a guide crossing the bridge with your audience, interacting with them face to face. If your audience pauses to ask about features of the bridge, their experience—and decision to cross—will be influenced by what you say and how you relate to them.

If you will be communicating in person, your primary medium is . . . you!

If you won't be there in person, your communication must stand alone to guide your audience across the bridge. Print is an obvious choice of medium—whether on paper or on screen—and if you choose to communicate electronically, you have the option of incorporating video and audio files.

However, there's a big difference between persuading in person and using a stand-alone communication.

In person, prioritize relationship and use slides that serve the audience

When you're face-to-face with your audience, persuasion starts with establishing trust and relationship, not with a slide deck. Too often, slides get in the way of personal interaction. The audience's relationship is not with your slides—it's with you! Well-designed slides enhance, but cannot replace, in-person presentation. The audience should be able to take them in as quickly as a drive-by billboard. Perhaps the one benefit of a slide that you're allowed as a presenter is that it serves as a cue to you, and as a clue to the audience, about what's coming next. Otherwise, if they're needed at all, slides should serve to do one or more of the following:

Build trust and belief.

Accelerate understanding.

Create useful associations.

Cue future action.

Build trust and belief. Seeing is believing. Slides are a powerful medium for delivering evidence that builds trust in the presenter and belief in the issues. Nothing says "quality problem!" more quickly or clearly than a photo of major defects in newly manufactured products, for example.

Accelerate understanding. Figure 19 presents the same data as a table and as a line graph. Were the data presented only as a table, it would take a few moments to realize that the general trend is upward. With a glance at the line graph, it's obvious. In this example, seeing the shape of the data reduces the audience's cognitive burden and accelerates their understanding.

Create useful associations. It's difficult for executives sitting at a beautifully polished table in San Francisco to imagine the challenges of transporting clinical samples in remote parts of Africa. "Sample transportation" would remain an abstract concept without an image like that in Figure 20.

This image immediately allows those executives see things in a stark, new light. In addition, this image puts everyone on the same page: infrastructure is an issue. Pairing abstract concepts with concrete images helps ensure that the audience "extracts uniform meaning from your message," says Carmen Simon.[37] She also notes that pictures are memorable when they're easy to label. The word "infrastructure" in Figure 20 is likely to stick.

TABLE

Jan	Feb	Mar	Apr	May	Jun
366	360	376	373	380	383

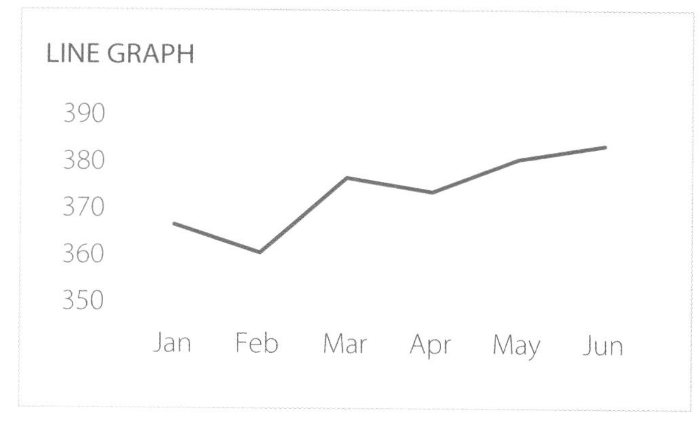

Figure 19: Use visuals that accelerate understanding

Cue future action. In situations where there's a delay between receiving your message and responding to the call to action, your audience needs a mental cue to act. To do so, they must first remember your message and anticipate sufficient rewards to take the desired action(s). An effective cue prompts actions such as, "When you see this, do that."

Here's an example of cueing future action: a training presentation for new laboratory janitorial staff introduces the biohazard symbol shown in Figure 21. This symbol serves as a cue to dress in protective clothing and to clean these areas differently from others.

Figure 20: Use images to create useful associations

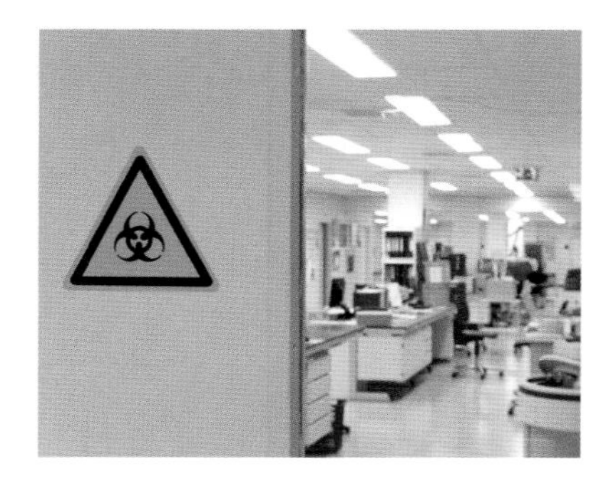

Figure 21: The biohazard symbol is a cue to behave differently

The primary reward in this case is the avoidance of pain: responding appropriately reduces their personal risk!

Consider the role of pre-reads

In some organizations, audiences expect presenters to send ahead the slide deck that will be used in the presentation as a "pre-read." Their intent is to be prepared, avoid unpleasant surprises, and get a sense of whether their time will be well spent. As a presenter, however, this puts you in a horrible jam because it implies that your slide deck should be able to stand alone. Slides designed to stand alone contain a lot more information than a drive-by billboard, so they will compete for your audience's attention during your own presentation! How can you build trust and relationship with people whose attention is divided?

Sending ahead an overcrowded slide deck is not the solution. Here are two alternatives.

Alternative 1. Create both a stand-alone pre-read and a full slide presentation. The pre-read will be a form of your strategic story designed for print or for an individual to read onscreen. First, build a slide deck based on your storyboard. Design clean, simple slides for the presentation: few words, readable fonts, clear visuals. Then, for the pre-read, select key graphics from that slide deck and support them with prose—full, punctuated sentences. Nancy Duarte coined the term "Slidedoc" to describe this type of communication.

Slidedocs, she says, are visual documents developed in presentation software that are intended to be read and referenced instead of projected.[38] Send *that* file ahead and use your slide deck to support your in-person presentation.

The pre-read will serve audience members who read it . . . but will everyone? Probably not. It's likely you'll end up presenting to a split audience: those who have read the pre-read and those who have not. To engage those who have read it, budget time for the questions that their reading is likely to have prompted. Also, provide them with richness in the form of additional examples and insights that supplement what they have read.

Alternative 2. Create a stand-alone pre-read and a few summary slides. This would work only where you can set the clear expectation that your audience will have read the pre-read in advance. The advantage of this approach is that you and your audience can use most of the presentation time for rich interaction. Practically, you would use the summary slides in the first few minutes to overview the key points of the pre-read such as the message, high-level arguments, and call to action. This serves as a reminder to those who have read the pre-read and provides face-saving cover for those who have not.[39] You can then use the rest of the time for questions, discussion, and decision-making. This gives you opportunities to build trust, relationships, and credibility with your audience, greatly enhancing your probability of success.

Be careful when reusing slides

As a rule: "Different audience, different story."

Have you ever sat through a presentation feeling that the speaker didn't understand your needs or the issue itself? Presenters who miss the mark lose credibility and face increasing resistance to their message.

Result: lose–lose.

One cause of this failure is that the presenter, under time pressure, reuses slides originally designed to support a different message. In fast-changing environments, using aged slides to convey a forward-looking message confuses and disappoints your audience. Another cause of failure is combining slides from various presentations that were designed to convey different messages to different audiences, months ago!

This doesn't mean that you can't use existing slides, but it does mean that you should do so thoughtfully. The danger in reusing a slide is that we tend to anchor on its content, thinking, "How can I use this?" instead of, "How can I best support my message to this audience?"

You can avoid this trap by first understanding your audience, then developing your message. As a rule: "Different audience, different story."

"Words and pictures are yin and yang. Married, they produce a progeny more interesting than either parent."[40]

—Theodor Seuss Geisel

AUTHOR OF DR. SEUSS CHILDREN'S BOOKS

Overview

The following two sections, "The seven steps" and "Key concepts and terms" serve as a one-stop, quick reference. You'll find this section helpful if you need a quick reminder of concepts, frequently used terms, or an overview of the process, without having to re-read sections of the book.

The seven steps

The wooden tiles included with the model Bridge outline Cruxio's seven-step process for building a strategic story—they summarize how to build a bridge.

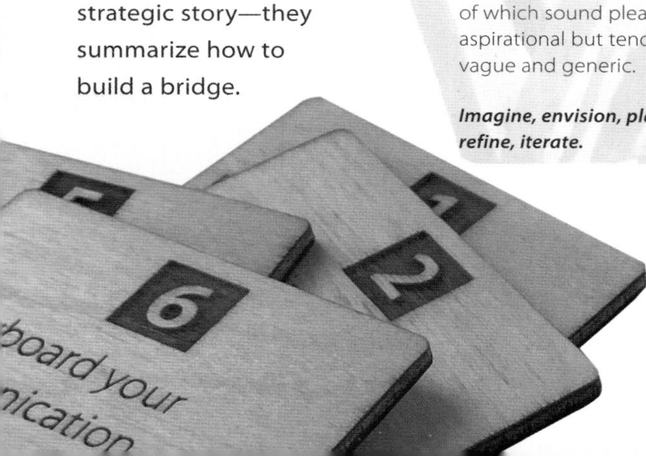

1

Envision the better future

Your current bridge is one of many on a longer-term, multi-stage journey to a better future.

By enabling others to envision this same future, you'll align expectations and action. You'll also ensure that your bridge is pointing in the right direction!

In this step, you develop photos or videos from the better future that suggest "If this is true, these other things must also be true." Envisioning in this way is more useful than through "vision statements," many of which sound pleasingly aspirational but tend to be vague and generic.

Imagine, envision, play, test, refine, iterate.

2

Empathize with your audience

The remaining steps focus on your current bridge, which will carry your audience to the next stage of the journey toward the better future.

Step two explores your audience's hopes and fears about that next move. It considers backdrop issues and assumptions that might color their current perspective. It asks what your audience will likely be thinking, feeling, and doing (if anything) related to your communication.

This step also asks how you can build trust and credibility with your audience because persuasion is founded on relationship.

Research, talk, empathize, analyze, question, care.

3

Select an achievable new perspective

Having considered your audience's backdrop and their current perspective, step three assesses how far they'll be willing to move toward the better future—how long your current bridge can be.

The audience will only cross your bridge if their perceived rewards for doing so outweigh their perceived risks.

Your goal in this step is to determine what you could *realistically* expect your audience to be thinking, feeling, and doing at the end of your strategic story: the new perspective you want them to adopt. You find this through an iterative process that assesses risks and rewards.

Experiment, empathize, analyze, test, iterate.

4

Develop message and arguments

In step four, you build a set of arguments and a message that will lead your audience to the new perspective.

This is a three-phase process. A divergent phase explores different sets of arguments. The convergent phase selects and refines one argument set. In the third phase, you derive the message from the final argument set.

The result is an outline of the strategic story's message supported by a pyramid of independent arguments, like this:

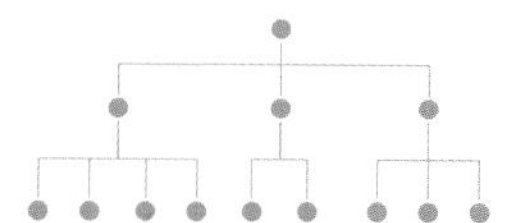

Question, play, structure, test, experiment, iterate.

5

Engaging opening; compelling closing

Step five outlines the opening that will clear the path to the message and arguments that you developed in step four. This opening must seize and direct your audience's attention in that direction.

This step also outlines how you'll close, having presented your message and arguments.

Once your audience has heard or read your arguments sequentially, your summary shows their combined strength. The closing may also include reminders of rewards and of the better future. It will always include an explicit call to action.

Play, imagine, test, experiment, iterate.

6

Storyboard your communication

The storyboard in step six maps the sequence of information through the opening, arguments, and closing.

It identifies the moment-to-moment sequence of data, facts, logic, and examples that comprise the complete strategic story.

Sequence matters at the level of the story's main arguments (the arches of the bridge) and at every level beneath them.

During storyboarding, you experiment with the intellectual and emotional effects of making small changes to the flow of information.

Structure, play, question, experiment, refine.

7

Select and prepare appropriate media

Step seven matches the communication medium—or media—to the audience's needs. Not every strategic story is a presentation supported by slides. Your bridge could be an important conversation, an email, or a document.

If you are presenting, you are the primary medium, not your slides, so prioritize relationship: it is the foundation of persuasion!

Question, simplify, test.

Key concepts and terms

Strategic Story

A strategic story is a persuasive communication that invites the audience to change its perspective and take specific action. It comprises three parts:

1. Opening
2. Arguments
3. Closing

1. Opening. The opening serves to engage and build a relationship with your audience. It clears a path to your message and its supporting arguments. The opening should take 5–15% of the story's time.

2. Arguments. Independent arguments support your message. Each argument comprises some or all of the following: data, facts, logic, and examples. The arguments take about 70–90% of the story's time.

3. Closing. Now that your audience has heard or read your arguments sequentially, begin your closing with a summary that shows their combined strength. The closing reminds the audience of their rewards for crossing the bridge. It may reintroduce the better future. It always includes a restatement of your message and a call to action. It typically takes 5–15% of the story's time.

The Cruxio Bridge represents one strategic story on a longer path toward a better future. To progress on that journey, the audience must cross the bridge and take action. They will only cross if their perceived rewards for doing so outweigh their risks.

Better Future

Strategic stories are designed to change a business by advancing toward a better future that you envision. In most cases, you want the audience to envision how that future will be better for them, too.

The better future will look different to different audiences. For example, in securing funding to get a drug to market, clinicians will be motivated by imagining the better future for patients. While investors may genuinely celebrate those benefits, the future they want to envision will be more directly related to the financial returns and kudos they earn for making a smart investment.

Getting to the top of the mountain (the better future) is usually a multi-stage journey that will require your audience to cross several bridges.

Backdrop

In theater, the stage is set against one or more backdrops that hang at the back of the set, providing context for the foreground action. Your audience will view your strategic story in the context of *their* backdrop, so it's important that you anticipate factors that could influence the success of your story.

The **backdrop** includes issues that may or may not be directly related to your communication.

Negative backdrop factors may inhibit the audience from stepping onto your bridge. "We've tried that before and it failed," is an example of a backdrop issue that's directly related to your proposal to move toward the better future. Other issues may be unrelated, such as budget cuts, competing priorities, or simply that the audience is tired, hungry, or distracted.

Backdrop factors can be positive, too. Examples include recent changes or events such as funding windfalls, favorable changes in the regulatory environment, or the support of a new leader.

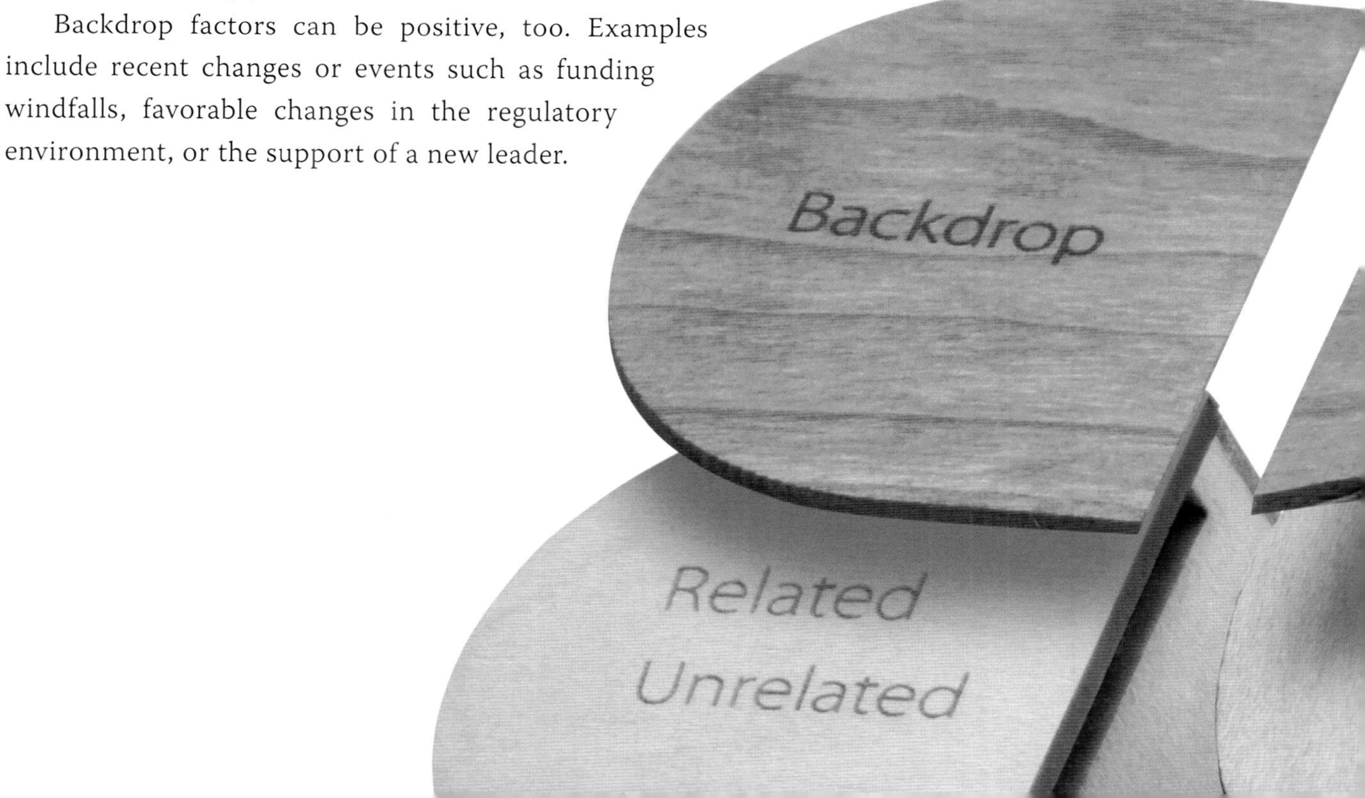

Current Perspective

At the opening of your communication, target audience members have their own thoughts and feelings about your anticipated message. They may be taking action in light of those expectations. To

The *current perspective* is marked on the road surface. The roadbed directly beneath reminds you to explore what your audience is likely to be *thinking, feeling,* and *doing* as they step onto your bridge.

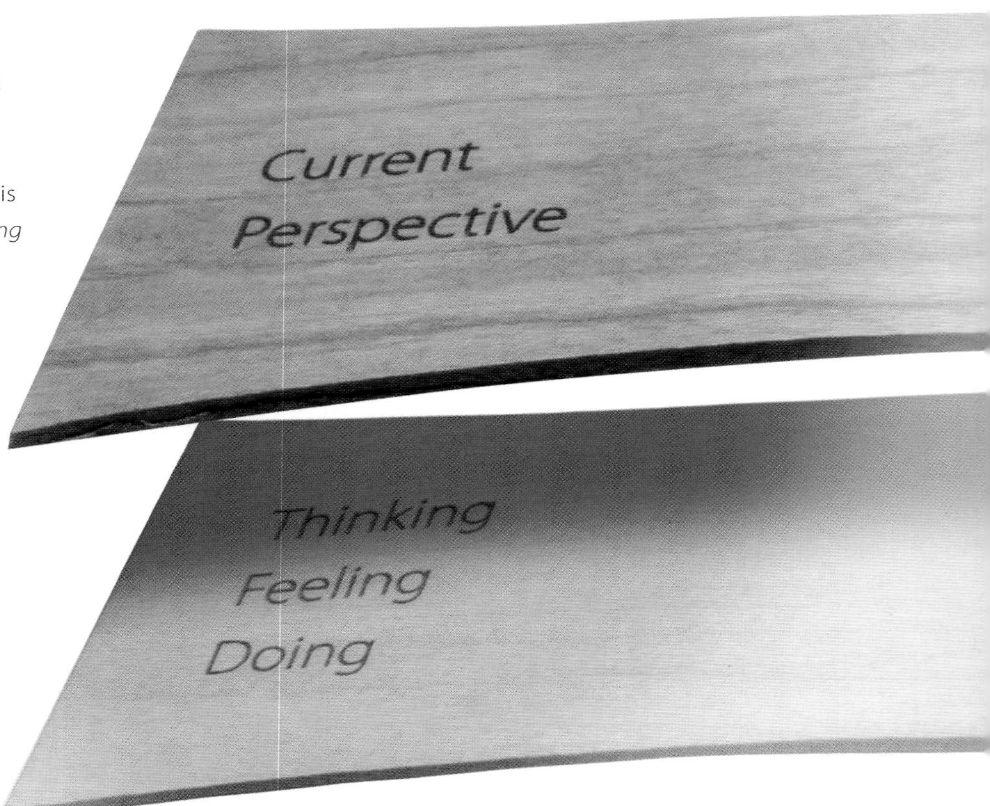

understand your audience's current perspective, consider the range of what your target audience is likely to be thinking, feeling, and doing (if anything), about moving toward the better future.

Engage, Connect, Frame

These terms relate to the opening of your communication. You need to *engage* the audience by seizing their attention and showing them why they should care about your message. *Connect* with

In opening, *engage* and *connect* with your audience before *framing* your message and its supporting arguments.

them personally. Demonstrate that you sincerely care about them. Empathize with them. During your opening you *frame* your message, in part, by raising a key question in your audience's minds.

Message

"*Message*" is printed on the roadbed, where it enables the audience's change in perspective on the road surface, above.

Your message answers a key question you have raised in your audience's minds (see, "Engage, Connect, Frame," on page 120). Your message, supported by independent arguments, carries the audience from their current perspective to the new perspective you want them to adopt.

The message has two important elements. First, it conveys your position, which could be as simple as recommending a course of action. Second, it conveys why your proposal or idea matters—or should matter—to the audience.

Arguments

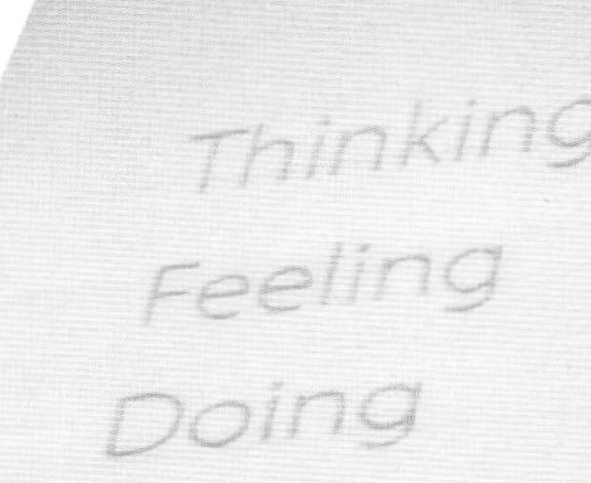

Independent arguments support your message. In the Cruxio Bridge model, they are the load-bearing arches of the bridge. When engineered well, they provide sufficient, but not excessive, support.

Your message is a short statement that answers a key question you have raised in your audience's minds. Each argument independently supports that answer. Arguments may include any or all of the following: data, facts, logic, and examples. "Examples" here is a broad term that encompasses such things as case studies, photos, videos, props, and narratives.

Message

Independent *arguments*—the arches of the bridge—support your message.

Argument 1, supported by data, facts, logic, and examples

Argument 2, supported by data, facts, logic, and examples

Argument 3, supported by data, facts, logic, and examples

New Perspective

The purpose of your communication is to move your audience to act because they have learned to see things differently. By crossing your bridge, they adopt a new perspective.

As you plan your strategic story, anticipate how your audience is likely to feel about moving toward the better future. They'll only cross your bridge if the rewards for doing so exceed their

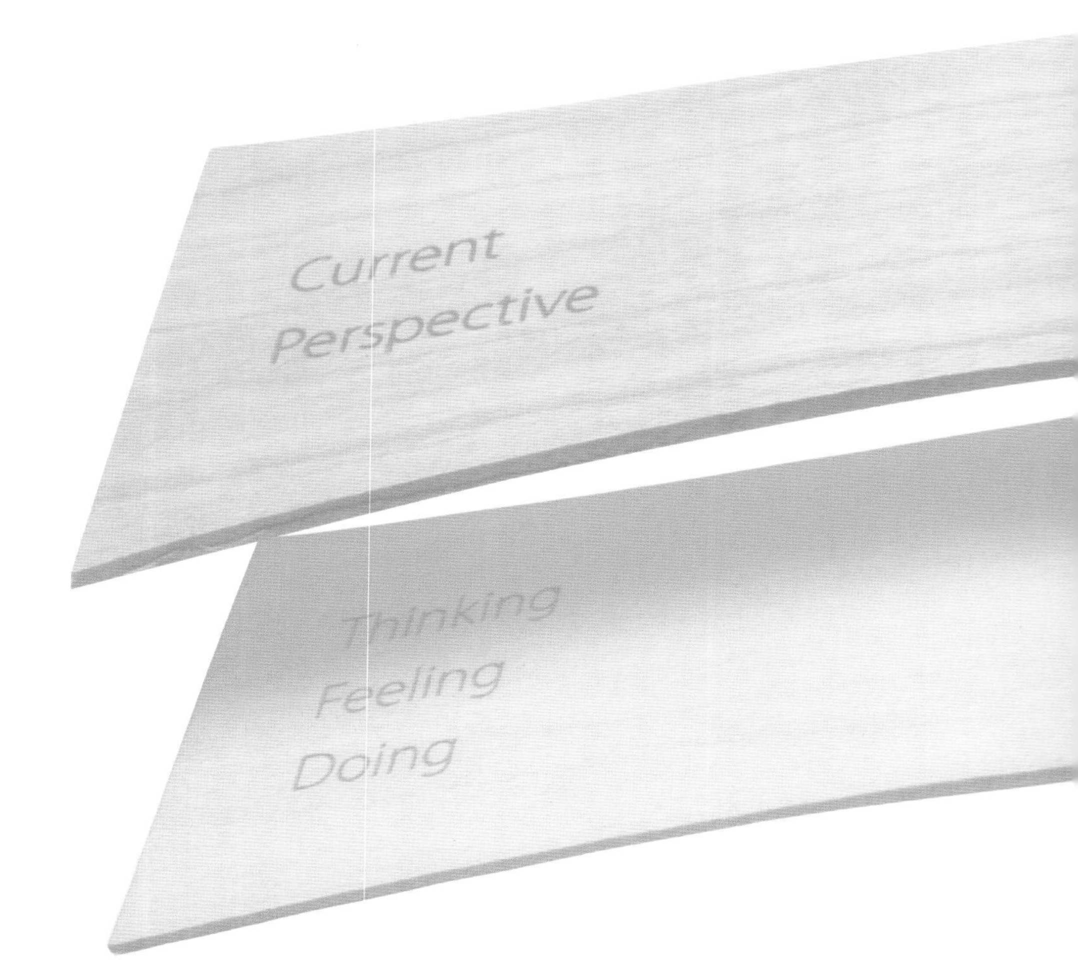

resistance. If you anticipate a lot of resistance, ask them to take a small step in that direction. You can ask them to take a bigger step if you anticipate less resistance or can offer more attractive rewards. Remember that rewards include both the hope of gain and the avoidance of pain.

The *new perspective* is marked on the road surface. The roadbed directly beneath reminds you to explore what you can reasonably expect the audience to be *thinking, feeling,* and *doing* at the end of your communication.

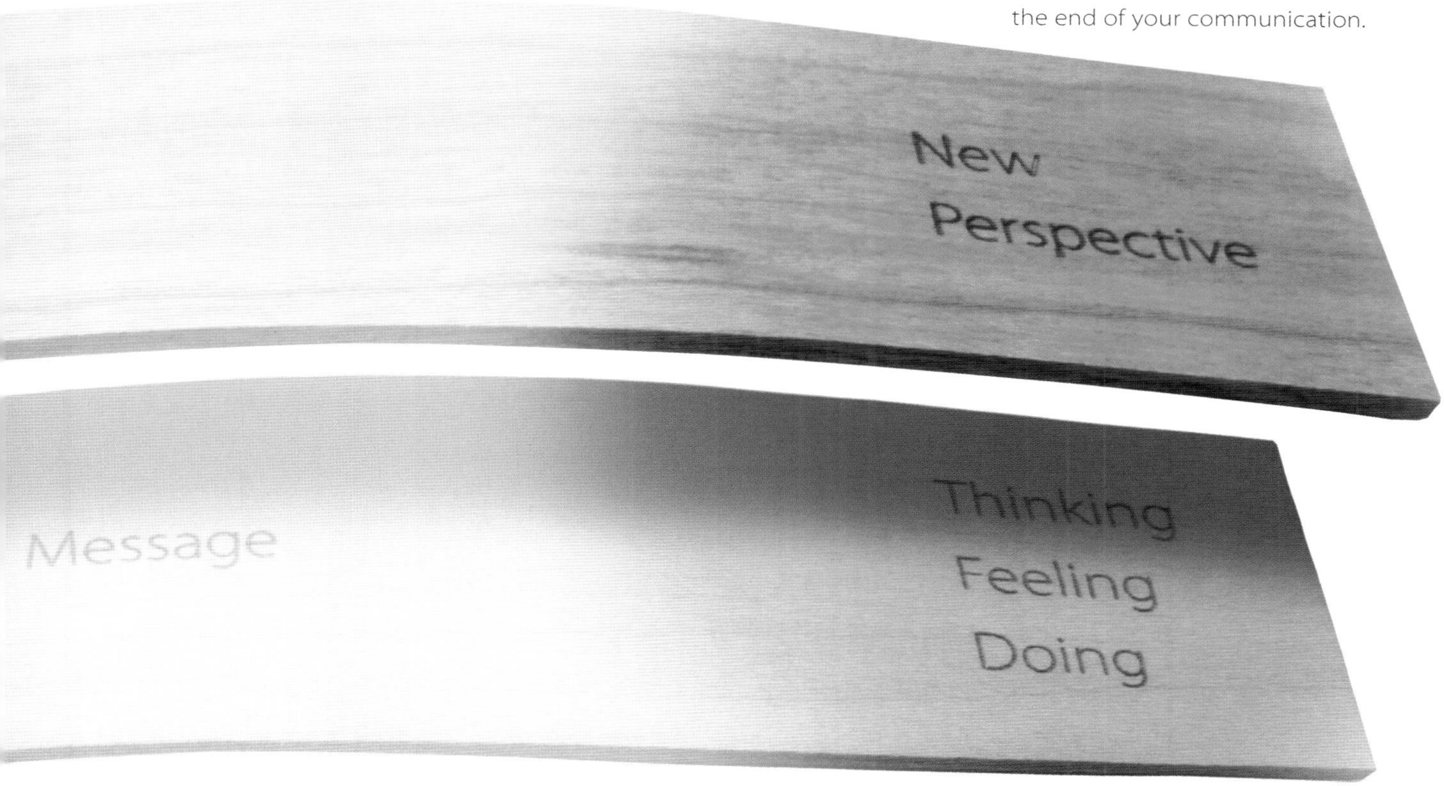

Summary

The summary is the beginning of your closing. Up to this point, your audience has heard (or read) your arguments sequentially, but they haven't had a chance to consider them collectively. Your summary ties the arguments together in support of your message.

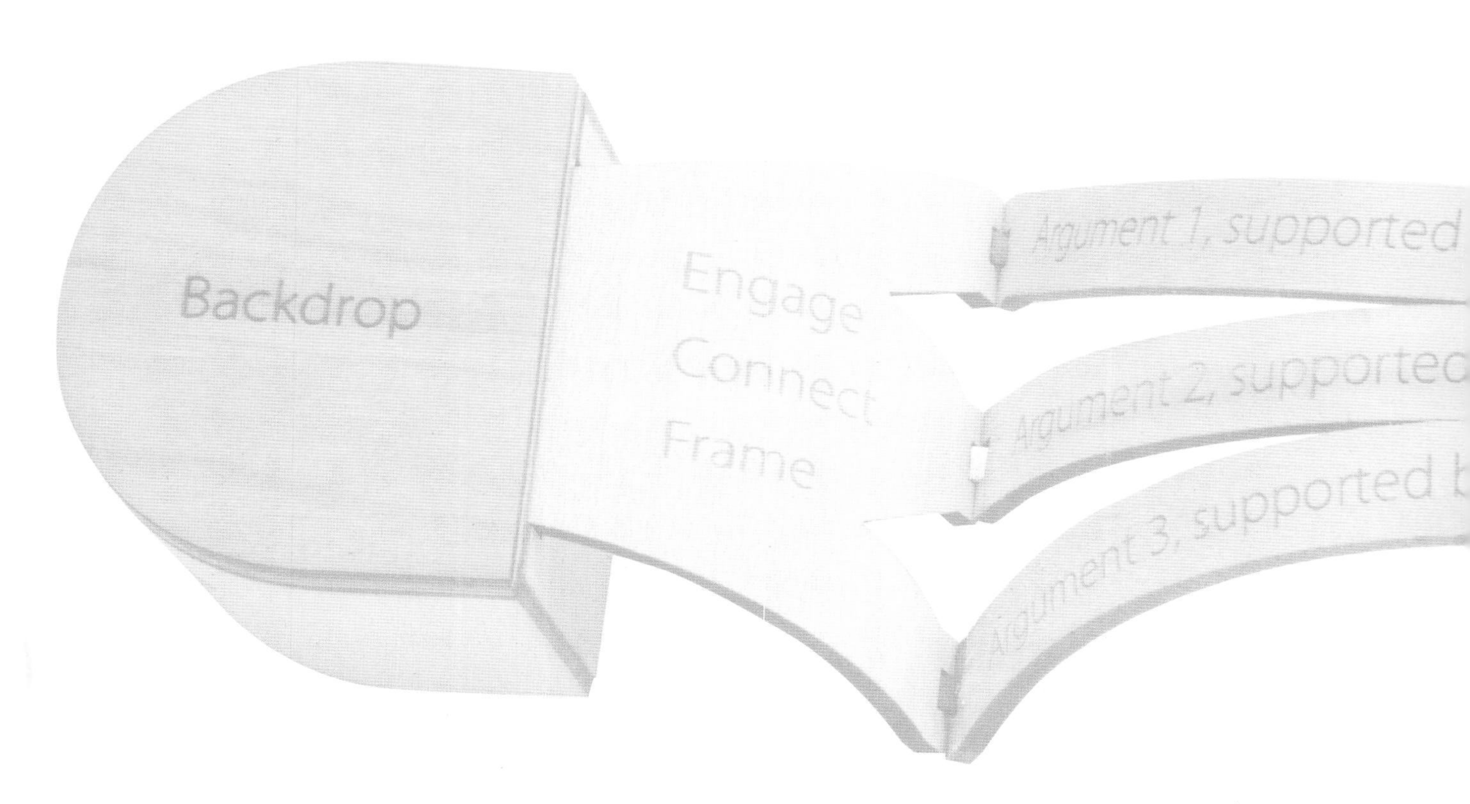

During your summary, you will usually remind your audience of their rewards for crossing this bridge: the potential for them to gain, avoid pain, or both. You will always state your message as a conclusion. It's often effective at this point to remind your audience of the better future you have helped them envision.

The ***summary*** ties the arguments together and reminds the audience of other rewards that merit adopting the new perspective.

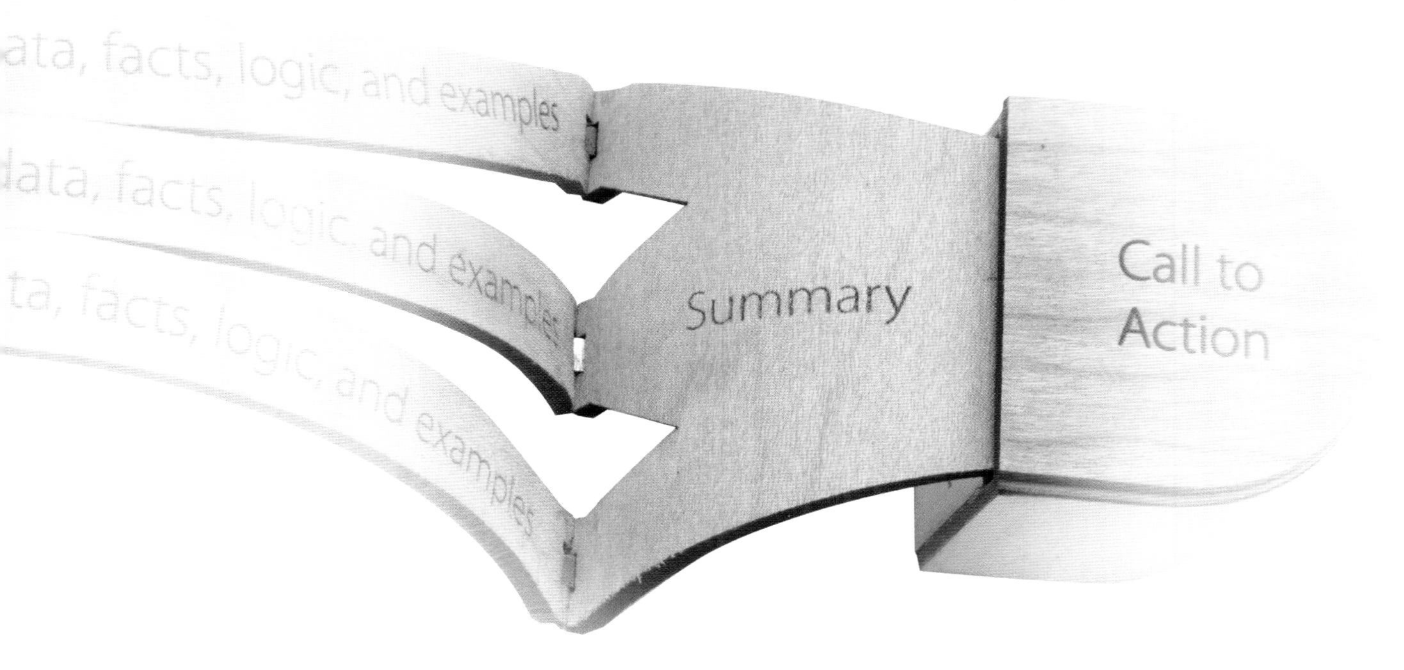

Call to Action

This is what you ask your audience to do at the end of your strategic story. These actions may be immediate or delayed. Examples of immediate action include approving funds for an initiative, scheduling the next meeting, or volunteering to help in specific ways. A delayed action could be an instruction for future use. For example, "When you see this problem, do this, not that."

Your *call to action* specifies what you want the audience to do. Action is the goal of every strategic story!

About the author

Rob Wishnowsky founded Cruxio, Inc., in 2005 to help business leaders get to the "crux" of their story. Before founding Cruxio, Rob headed the Biochemicals division of Boehringer Mannheim in Australia, and held leadership roles in sales, marketing, and strategy for Roche and Johnson and Johnson in the US.

Today, Rob leads workshops and coaches business leaders in strategic story development and delivery. His work with several of the world's leading pharmaceutical companies, clinical diagnostic manufacturers, and emerging drug discovery companies has helped executives secure, collectively, more than $5 billion in funding.

Rob holds a bachelor's degree in microbiology from Otago University in New Zealand and a master's degree in marketing from the University of Technology, Sydney. He is known for taking creative approaches to business problems, which is influenced by his background in the performing arts and music. Rob lives in the San Francisco Bay area, where he still jams with friends on the piano, guitar, harmonica, and wind instruments.

Notes

1. The Investor's Field Guide, "Buffett wisdom that you may not have heard before," http://investorfieldguide.com/2015122buffett-wisdom-that-you-may-not-have-heard-before/.
2. The Nobel Prize, "Daniel Kahneman Facts," https://www.nobelprize.org/prizes/economic-sciences/2002/kahneman/facts/.

   Although he is a psychologist, Kahneman won the Nobel Prize in economics for "having integrated insights from psychological research into economic science, especially concerning human judgment and decision-making under uncertainty."
3. Daniel Kahneman, *Thinking, Fast and Slow* (New York: Farrar, Straus and Giroux, 2011), Kindle, under, "1. The Characters of the Story."

   Kahneman describes two modes of thinking: one is slow and deliberate, the other is very fast and subconscious. The slow mode "has beliefs, makes choices, and decides what to think about and what to do." The fast mode, he says, effortlessly originates impressions and feelings "that are the main sources of the explicit beliefs and deliberate choices" that we attribute to the slow mode.

4. Braithwaite Communications, "How Daniel Kahneman learned the value of stories." July 24, 2017, https://gobraithwaite.com/thinking/how-daniel-kahneman-learned-the-value-of-stories-for-thinking-fast-and-slow/.
5. arsTECHNICA, "Testing Leonardo da Vinci's bridge: His design was stable, study finds," October 16, 2019, https://arstechnica.com/science/2019/10/testing-leonardo-da-vincis-bridge-his-design-was-stable-study-finds/.
6. National Geographic, "Leonardo's Bridge: Part 2. 'A Bridge for the Sultan,'" January 22, 2013, https://blog.nationalgeographic.org/2013/01/22/leonardos-bridge-part-2-a-bridge-for-the-sultan/.

   This article translates a portion of a letter from da Vinci to the sultan in which he describes the bridge as follows: "I, your faithful servant, understand that it has been your intention to erect a bridge from Galata (Pera) to Stambul . . . across the Golden Horn ("Haliç"), but this has not been done because there were no experts available. I, your subject, have determined how to build the bridge. It will be a masonry bridge as high as a building, and even tall ships will be able to sail under it."
7. arsTECHNICA, "Testing Leonardo da Vinci's bridge."

   This well-illustrated article outlines MIT research demonstrating that da Vinci's arched masonry design would have worked and that it incorporated abutments that provided stability in the earthquake-prone region.

8. Carmen Simon, *Impossible to Ignore: Creating Memorable Content to Influence Decisions,* (New York: McGraw-Hill Education, 2016), 153, 246.

   In this fascinating, accessible book, Dr. Simon lists 15 variables that we can use to influence others' memory. One of these variables is "sensory intensity"—the degree to which our senses are activated when we are exposed to a stimulus. Simon comments on the role of the senses in well-crafted stories, noting " . . . a good story invokes more senses and activates more parts of the brain: visual cortex, motor cortex, frontal cortex, amygdala, to name a few. As a result, when we tell a story well—especially if we lived the events ourselves—we can help *others* encode more memory traces."

9. Sean Vitousek, "On the bridge," http://www.pelicannetwork.net/bigsur-bixby-bridge/.

   This paper states that the Bixby Bridge cost just $199,861 in 1932. Using the calculator at MeasuringWorth.com, this equates to $3.74 million 2019 dollars based on the Consumer Price Index (https://www.measuringworth.com/calculators/uscompare/).

10. Leonard Safir and William Safire (editors), *Good Advice,* (NYT Times Books, New York, 1982), 44.
11. Peter Drucker, *The Essential Drucker: Selections from the Management Works of Peter F. Drucker* (New York: Harper Business, 2001), 271.
12. CNN Business, "Bill Gates' 40th anniversary email: Goal was 'a computer on every desk,'" April 6, 2015, https://money.

cnn.com/2015/04/05/technology/bill-gates-email-microsoft-40-anniversary/index.html.

13. John F. Kennedy: NASA, "The Decision to Go to the Moon," https://history.nasa.gov/moondec.html.

    Dr. Martin Luther King: Stanford University, "'I Have a Dream,' Address Delivered at the March on Washington for Jobs and Freedom," https://kinginstitute.stanford.edu/king-papers/documents/i-have-dream-address-delivered-march-washington-jobs-and-freedom.

    Anita Roddick: Quotations by Women.com, https://quotationsbywomen.com/authorq/27305/.

14. Inc.com, "Jeff Bezos Says Your Most Important Decisions in Life Should Always Be Made This Way (but It Will Make Many Uncomfortable)," https://www.inc.com/marcel-schwantes/jeff-bezos-says-your-most-important-decisions-in-life-should-always-be-made-this-way-but-it-will-make-many-uncomfortable.html.

15. CDC, "Interim Estimates of 2019–20 Seasonal Influenza Vaccine Effectiveness—United States, February 2020," February 21, 2020, https://www.cdc.gov/mmwr/volumes/69/wr/mm6907a1.htm.

16. Robert Cialdini, *Pre-Suasion: A Revolutionary Way to Influence and Persuade* (New York: Simon and Schuster, 2016), Kindle, under, "1: Pre-Suasion: An Introduction."

    On trust: "Trust is one of those qualities that leads to compliance with requests, provided that it has been planted before the request is made."

On being like another person: "There is a certain type of unity—of identity—that best characterizes a *We* relationship and that, if pre-suasively raised to consciousness, leads to more acceptance, cooperation, liking, help, trust, and consequently, assent."

17. Robert Cialdini, *Influence: Science and practice (Fourth ed.)* (Massachusetts: Allyn and Bacon, 2001), 143–156.

    On liking: In *Influence*, Professor Cialdini identifies six universal principles of persuasion. Liking is one of them. The planned sequel to this Quick-Start Guide, *Bridge-Building Insights,* will outline these six universal principles, and a seventh universal principle that he added in *Pre-Suasion.*

18. Rare Book Room, "Benjamin Franklin," http://www.rarebookroom.org/Control/frapoq/index.html.
19. Daniel Kahneman and Amos Tversky. Prospect Theory: An Analysis of Decision under Risk. *Econometrica*, 47(4) (1979): 263–291.

    Loss aversion was first identified by Amos Tversky and Daniel Kahneman in 1979. It describes our preference to avoid losses over acquiring equivalent gains.

20. Daniel Kahneman and Amos Tversky, A. Advances in prospect theory: Cumulative representation of uncertainty. *Journal of Risk and Uncertainty*, 5(4), (October 1992): 297–323.

    This later research suggested that avoidance of loss is twice as powerful as equivalent gain.

21. Robert Cialdini, "Pre-Suasion," under "Social Proof."

This leverages one of Dr. Cialdini's six universal principles of persuasion called "social proof" or "consensus." According to this principle, we look to others like ourselves to determine how to think or act, especially when we're uncertain.

22. Nancy Duarte, *Slide:ology: The Art and Science of Creating Great Presentations,* (California: O'Reilly Media, 2008), 13.
23. John Medina, *Brain Rules,* (Seattle: Pear Press, 2014), 123.
24. Barbara Minto, *The Pyramid Principle: Logic in Writing and Thinking (Third Ed.),* (London: Prentice Hall, 2002).
25. Jean-luc Doumont, *Trees, maps, and theorems: Effective communication for rational minds,* (Belgium: Principiae, 2009), 3.
26. Simon, *Impossible to Ignore,* 151-153.
27. Simon, *Impossible to Ignore,* 60.

    One way to make a message more memorable is to link it to people's own thoughts. This reflective attention makes your point, message, or example more memorable.

28. Simon, *Impossible to Ignore,* 93.

    Dr. Simon distinguishes between expectation (the meeting will begin at 3 p.m.) and anticipation (the amount of your annual bonus will be revealed during the meeting). Anticipation, which is about *feeling* the future, provides a stronger incentive to act than does expectation. An invitation to imagine something draws on our past experiences while stimulating both anticipation and emotion. This powerful combination can help push people to action.

29. Oddvar Holmseland, *A Critical Introduction to Henry Green's Novels,* (New York: Palgrave Macmillan, 1986), 239.
30. Simon, *Impossible to Ignore*, 2.
31. Nielson Norman Group, "The Peak-End Rule: How Impressions Become Memories," December 30, 2018, https://www.nngroup.com/articles/peak-end-rule/.
32. Dorothy Sarnoff, *Speech can Change your Life*, (New York: Dell, 1971), 217.
33. Nancy Duarte, *Resonate: Present Visual Stories that Transform Audiences*, (New Jersey: Wiley, 2010), 36–51.
34. Simon, *Impossible to Ignore*, 72.
35. Simon, *Impossible to Ignore*, 77–78.
36. Chip Heath and Dan Heath, *Made to Stick*, (New York: Random House, 2007), 106.
37. Simon, *Impossible to Ignore*, 164.
38. Nancy Duarte, "Slidedocs®: Spread Ideas with Visual Documents," https://www.duarte.com/slidedocs/.
39. Slab.com, "How Jeff Bezos Turned Narrative into Amazon's Competitive Advantage," February 5, 2019, https://slab.com/blog/jeff-bezos-writing-management-strategy/.

    Jeff Bezos, Amazon's founder, offers another worthwhile alternative. He banned his team's use of PowerPoint and bullet lists in 2004. Instead, people communicate through densely written, multi-page, narrative memos. According to this article, Bezos "often holds a silent meeting, where senior leaders read these memos prior to starting a discussion."

Here's how Bezos explained his thinking in an email on June 9, 2004:

> "The reason writing a good 4-page memo is harder than 'writing' a 20-page PowerPoint is because the narrative structure of a good memo forces better thought and better understanding of what's more important than what, and how things are related.
>
> "PowerPoint-style presentations somehow give permission to gloss over ideas, flatten out any sense of relative importance, and ignore the interconnectedness of ideas."

40. Quote Investigator, "Words and Pictures are Yin and Yang," https://quoteinvestigator.com/2014/03/20/yin-yang/#return-note-8460-1.

This site attributes the source to a longer version of this quote published in the Dartmouth Alumni Magazine, Volume 68, Number 8, April 1976, in which Theodor Seuss Geisel is quoted as saying:

> "I began to get it through my skull that words and pictures were Yin and Yang. I began thinking that words and pictures, married, might possibly produce a progeny more interesting than either parent. It took me almost a quarter of a century to find the proper way to get my words and pictures married. At Dartmouth, I couldn't even get them engaged."

Index

Page numbers followed by *e, f, n* indicate an example, figure, or note, respectively.

Cruxio Training

Cruxio's purpose is to equip businesspeople to persuade others. So, in addition to creating strategic stories with clients, we coach executives through the Cruxio Bridge process and offer a range of training programs for individuals, teams, and organizations. The following three workshops anchor our broader training services. For more information about our corporate programs, workshops, coaching, and short deep-dive clinics, visit www.cruxio.com/training.

Persuasion Strategy

One day, two half-days, or four two-hour interactive virtual sessions.

Apply the Cruxio Bridge process and principles to real stories submitted by workshop participants. You'll receive a copy of this book* and your own wooden model Cruxio Bridge kit as a hands-on, visual reminder of strategic story structure. Your experience in this workshop will accelerate and strengthen your ability to craft your own persuasive strategic stories.

*Alternatively, you can credit the value of this book against the course fee by quoting your unique code on the next page when you register. Each code may be credited toward the course fee only once.

Persuasion Tactics

One day, two half-days, or four two-hour interactive virtual sessions.

Learn tradecraft that will make your robust, persuasive, strategic story more compelling. Emotions and unconscious mental processes influence decisions far more than most people realize—even in the rational world of business! This workshop reveals how you can overcome emotional and cognitive barriers to action, enhancing your probability of success.

All Eyes on You

One day or two half-days of interactive sessions in person.

Using your eyes, body, and voice effectively can be powerfully persuasive, whether you're presenting virtually or in person. In this workshop, you'll learn and practice skills in a live presentation environment because, while the principles behind these skills translate effectively into the virtual environment, they are best learned and practiced in person.

B-2035

Your unique code